THE HELL OF
SOCIAL
PHOBIA

THE HELL OF
SOCIAL
PHOBIA

by
Terry Cunningham
© 2008

First published 2005
by Stagedoor Publishing
London WC1N 3XX UK

Revised, Enlarged 2nd Edition Published 2008

www.zoism.co.uk

ISBN 0 9521620 7 5

This book is dedicated
to those who suffer
the pain and misery
of phobias

Other publications by the same author include:

Travels on the Hound
South Across the River
The Great 78's
The President Demands Maximum Attack
Geronimo's Cadillac
Pacific Graveyard
14 –18. The Final Word
Bram Stoker's Irving
The Timeless James Dean

Contents

Foreword

I first met Steve Conway back in the 1980s, when my editor had asked me to write an article about people who suffered from strange or little-known medical conditions.

Over the next couple of months, I visited several hospitals and met many different types of highly qualified medical staff who explained to me the disastrous effects these conditions have on the lives of their patients. For some reason back then, the victims of social phobia never discussed their problems and tried to fool the world – and themselves – that all was well. This did not help them, nor the public perception of this miserable illness and the many other very similar phobias and equally crushing conditions.

With the passing years and the advent of the internet social phobia has become more widely known, although in most cases the cause remains a mystery.

I have to admit my own ignorance back in those days because, when the doctor asked me to come and meet some of his patients, I was expecting to encounter some very unbalanced retarded people.

I was in for some heavy enlightenment.

The people I met were all very pleasant once you got through their initial shyness, and all intelligent – some I would class as highly so. The only common denominator that I suppose I was looking for was that they were mostly the sensitive type. Apart from that they were from all walks of life, of both sexes and of all ages. Over a period of many weeks I had in-depth interviews with more than fifty of them, including Steve and his two friends, Lisa and Jack.

I've been re-reading my old notes and have been reminded of the man who worked as a steeplejack...heights didn't bother him, but dogs did! He had a total phobia about them; if he saw someone walking a toy poodle he would collapse with fear, fighting for his breath. So, together with the doctors, I took this brave man for a day out to Battersea Dogs Home...to confront his fear, head on. (Famous in London as an organisation that takes in stray and unwanted dogs, the public goes to Battersea Dogs Home to choose a new pet.)

As we got out of the car the sound of so much barking from inside the building made the poor man pass out before he'd even seen a dog. The doctor wisely decided that to continue could have brought on a heart attack. So, for the rest of his life, this man lived in terror of seeing a dog around the next corner. My first question to him was, 'Were you ever bitten by a dog as a child?' The answer was, 'No, never.'

How about London buses? Yes, the big red double-decker ones you see on every main street in the capital. One woman, who was by profession a lawyer, had a phobia about them; she could never get on one. Even the sight of one would terrify her to the extent of making her ill. So she had to alter her entire life and move out of London to where the local transport company ran differently coloured buses. A bus that was not red she had no fear of.

'OK. So did anything bad happen to you on a bus at some time?' Her answer: 'No, never.'

I was starting to realise the difficult task the doctors were facing.

When I presented my finished work to the editor his reaction was, to say the very least, backward and compassionless. 'Oh, come on, why would anyone be scared of a bus unless it was about to run you over, or a dog unless it was about to bite you?' The one that really threw him was why the hell anyone would not want to go to a party.

In my mind's eye I could see again those poor souls at the clinic shaking uncontrollably as they stood in front of their fellow sufferers trying to say a few words and then, when mental confusion set in, drying up completely and stumbling back to their seats.

'Never judge a man until you have walked a mile in his shoes,' I told him. If he didn't like it, so what. I've been sacked before. But, to his credit, he did print it and it got a great response from the readers.

About a year ago the new editor, a woman, asked me to do a follow-up to see how the original fifty had faired. For the most part it was a sad experience. Seventeen of those good people had died, eleven of them by their own hand. A few told me they had improved, but only provided they kept strictly to the strong medication that had been prescribed and kept in touch with their clinics.

Only Steve would I class as cured and now living a normal life.

When he asked me to write his story I was reluctant, because I pointed out that books about illness are always written by doctors of one sort or another. 'That,' he said, 'is why this will be original and very unusual. Let me, the patient and sufferer, tell it from my side and I'll hold nothing back. Then all those trying to deal with social phobia out there will know they are not alone and they can get well, as I did, no matter how long they have had to endure it.'

So, apart from changing the names of all the medical people, I've let Steve tell his strange and poignant story in his own words. I know it will show social phobia to the public in a new light, and people will see that we are talking about a life-long illness with the most dreadful long- lasting effects.

As Steve sadly told me, he can never get those lost years back; but if his story stops just one person heading down the same path, then it's the best thing he ever did.

Terry Cunningham

Welcome, My Friend

Yes, we are friends, because there's a bond between us. We both know the *hell* of suffering "social phobia" or, as in my case, "severe social phobia".

To make it easier, from now on I will call it **SP**, for short.

It matters not if you are a man or a woman, nor if you are young or old. If you suffer the crippling fear of *SP* then this book could help you more than anything has ever done before, and I promise you the only side-effects from it will be positive ones.

We are not talking here of being worried about going for that job interview or being rather nervous because you've been asked to make a speech at your friend's wedding.

No. You have to be a sufferer of severe *SP* to know or understand the pure terror that a victim of this illness feels. It's the sort of blind panic, pure terror and mind numbing fear that one would feel if facing a firing squad or if you fell into a lion's cage.

You shake like a leaf, your face goes bright red, your mouth is so dry that you can't speak and your legs turn to jelly. Your thoughts are confused and disorientated. Forget butterflies in the stomach; your guts are twisted inside out with *fear*. And your ultimate wish is to be anywhere on earth but the place you're at right now.

What makes it even worse – if that's possible – is that *in your heart you know there is nothing to be scared of.*

I felt just like that every day for years, but what puzzled me was that when I was in a room alone I had none of those feelings. My hands were perfectly steady, I didn't blush, and my thoughts would be clear and collected, but even in the safety of my room I was always worried and anxious about some trivial thing – a meeting I had to go to or someone I had to see – so I lived a life of constant fear and anxiety.

If you experience that on a daily basis with no end to it in sight, then you have a terrible burden: one that other people never have to face and can't really understand.

SP is the most savage of all phobias, disabling the sufferer completely.

All phobias are dreadful, but what if, for example, you have a phobia about snakes? Well, how often do you have to face one if you live in a city?

I did a survey with an *SP* society with 255 members who tried it over six months: the result was an 89 per cent success rate. I am very proud of that.

I was even more proud of the many who got up in the hall to say how much better their lives were.

Then I stood up and made a short thank-you speech, even got a polite round of applause.

There were a few tears shed that night, but what the hell. We made it, didn't we? We're entitled to our tears, tears of joy.

So, a cure worked on and devised by a fellow sufferer of long-standing. That must surely be the very best recommendation.

I've no axe to grind. All I want is for you to feel better and to put an end to your mental torment.

I know far better than most how you're feeling.

Right now, you're sitting in your lonely, dark, fear-filled room, feeling full of dread and petrified about facing something that others would regard as trivial.

But not to you is it a job interview, going somewhere, making a speech, any type of social occasion.

That room you're in may be a real room where you live or that poor miserable room inside your head. Let's face it: that's where we all really do live – in our mind with our thoughts.

Well, I have come to the door of your room and flung it wide open. It's bright sunshine outside with a clear blue sky and via this book I'm reaching out my hand to you saying, 'Grab, hold, trust me. I'll lead you out of there.'

Remember, I've lived in this room too, for far longer than you have.

When you first get outside you'll feel shaky; you're not used to the bright sun, so take some deep breaths of that great fresh air.

Each day now, you will get stronger.

The alternative is too awful to contemplate. You could stay in that room and get slowly worse. In fact, it's not a room at all; it's a prison cell.

So, OK, I've got your hand tight. We're on our way out. Kick the door shut behind you with a bang.

Now that I know you, let me introduce myself.

I'm a guy who suffered severe *SP* for nearly all my adult years. It took away my life.

The Start of a 40 Year Nightmare

My earliest symptoms started around the age of fifteen, in my last year at school, when I became very self-conscious and developed a fearful dread of being asked to read in front of the class. When this happened my hands would shake as I held the book I was reading from. My mouth would go so dry I could hardly speak and I dared not look up at my audience, the sight of all those faces staring at me was petrifying.

Apart from that, as a school boy I was OK. I played football for the school team and was in the boxing club (I usually got knocked out of the ring in the first round). It was harmless schoolboy stuff; no one ever got hurt and we had some laughs.

I had pals, no one ever tried to push me around, but there was always that deep-down feeling of anxiety.

I tried to have fun and, I suppose, be happy, but for some unknown reason I was worried and scared. If you'd asked me what I was worried and scared about, I couldn't come up with an answer. A constant state of extreme anxiety is one hell of a thing to live with.

Being interested in clothing and fashion, I started work in the tailoring trade. I went each day into London's West End and was employed in a small workshop. There were only two or three other workers; you had to concentrate intently on the work, so there was very little talking. It was quite and genteel way of life, but the only people you came in contact with were those who called to collect the finished garments. So, not much they're in the way of meeting and mixing with people.

I also attended day colleges and evening schools, but they were an ordeal, to say the least. I would always find a seat at the back of the class so as not to be noticed, and many a time I wanted to ask the lecturer a question but never had the nerve, knowing that all the class would turn to look at who had asked it and see this idiot with the bright red face stuttering and trembling, tongue-tied and embarrassed.

I tried not to admit it to myself, but I knew something was seriously wrong with me.

Remembering Famous Friends

The stories about Frank Sinatra's bad behaviour are legendary, so when Cyril, the owner of the firm, got a call from Frank's P.A to say he was on his way over, we got ready for trouble. However, from the minute he sauntered into the shop one bright afternoon, accompanied by a couple of minders, there was nothing but good vibes. Cyril introduced me as his 'top cutter and fashion designer', flattering but a bit O.T.T. Frank just said 'hi'. I found him business like but charming.

I was expecting my *SP* to go into overdrive dealing with this world famous entertainer, who at that time was one of the top recording artists and movie stars on the planet, but no. It was there of course, like always, but for some inexplicable reason it stayed fairly low volume.

I showed him lengths of our finest and highly expensive materials. He talked quietly about the vicuña sports jacket he wanted plus some formal suits and stage suits. For the stage I suggested lightweight silk worsted because it has a sheen to it that looks great under the spotlights. He sat next to me as I drew some sketches of the type of styles I thought would be right for him. My hands shook slightly but nowhere near as bad as they usually did when drawing in front of customers. I know he noticed this but he said nothing.

Frank knew to the last detail how he wanted his clothes to look. Coffee was brought in by May, our office girl, who told him her favourite recording of his was "My One and Only Love". He said it was a number he was fond of too, because of the lyrics. He was very nice to her and signed her autograph book. She walked away in a daze clutching the book tight.

One of his minders had stationed himself by the door, the other one was hovering close to Frank. At one point he turned to them saying; 'you guys can take it easy and put your arses to anchor' (I assumed that meant take a seat).

'I've told you', he continued, 'English fans are OK, you don't get the crazies over here that you get out on the west coast' (I don't think he'd say that now, but it was probably true back then).

After being with us for close to two hours he stood up to leave. Whilst Cyril was arranging when it would be

Sinatra's.' I heard some time later that Cyril made that trip and had a great time, Frank was a super host.

There were many other customers who were World famous at that time, but are mostly forgotten now. Many of them I knew well and socialised with. I'll tell you about some that still haunt me, if that's the right word (and I think it is, as you'll see).

Two movie stars I did not want to mix with were Rex Harrison and Stewart Granger. They were both very nasty to deal with; rude, arrogant and difficult. They were also very slow to pay their bills, so much so that Cyril told them to take their business elsewhere.

Women wore tailored costumes and skirts back then, so we had several famous lady customers. Two that I recall with affection were Alma Cogan and Diana Dors.

Alma was a singer and star of TV and radio; she would often come in with John Lennon of the Beatles, they were an item at the time. He never bought anything and I found him to be sarcastic. Also, I didn't like the way he talked down to people. She was a very sexy lady and a lovely person to chat to.

One day, when she came in, she forgot her latest LP that she had promised to give me. So, she called at my flat to give it to me and we spent a pleasant evening over coffee, listening to her LP. I mentioned that the staff at the shop didn't like Lennon. She said that you must allow for people like John; they have been very rich and famous since they were teenagers, they know nothing about the real world or doing a day's work, being broke or paying bills. They're surrounded by people who take care of their every need, and nobody ever says no to them. She had a good point; I found stars that had lived an ordinary life before hitting the big time much nicer to deal with.

Movie star Diana Dors was a real gem. It's not professional of me but I admit I looked forward to taking her measurements; she was one very sexy lady. One day she came in on the same day singer Tommy Steele came in to try on his wedding suit. The shop was full of press and TV cameras. She whispered to me; 'Steve, get me out of this, I don't have proper make up on.'

We went to the workroom at the back of the shop where she sat drinking tea and chatting to me and the rest of the staff about movies. She was often accompanied by phone me and say 'please make it my way'. I did, because he was the one who was going to wear it.

My reason for remembering Paul Getty, reputed to be the richest man in the World, is because he never made any conversation, was very distant and was so miserable and unhappy I almost felt sorry for him. He gave off an air of total depression. Almost every day I had to deal with someone World famous at that time. This became impossible for me because of my *SP*, but it also taught me that money and fame do not make for happiness, or peace of mind.

One last person I must mention from that time of my life, because I hope you'll find his story interesting, was a doctor. He was a charming, polite man with a melodious and soothing speaking voice that any actor would die for. In fact, as soon as he spoke my *SP* would subside slightly. He was Doctor Stephen Ward (a name that today is still surrounded in mystery).

On this occasion I was having a hellish *SP* day, I'd already seen several customers and couldn't get the shaking, stuttering and blushing under control. He came in to try on a suit he had ordered. As I wrote some details about his clothes in my order book, he noticed my hands trembling. With his rather elegant way of talking, he said; 'my dear chap, you're suffering from extreme anxiety. Do call round and see me, I can help.'

He had a medical practice just a short walk away, near the BBC. Later that week, feeling desperate, I took him up on his offer. He told me that he had studied medicine in America, where he had qualified as a doctor, but here in London he practiced holistic and homeopathic medicine, and was a qualified osteopath and masseur. He started by massaging my neck, head and shoulders and told me my muscles were locked tight with tension. He went on to explain that this was causing my constant painful headaches. He was very skilled and I found it relaxing, and by the second visit my headaches were gone.

'Now,' he said, 'try and tell me why you're in such a state?'

He had several deep, comfortable armchairs around the room so I sank into one while he poured a couple of Sherries. He sat back listening intently as I tried to explain my *SP,* and the devastating effect it was having on my life.

who was sleeping with John Profumo, the Nation's War Minister, as well as a Russian spy. So what had she told the Russian's about Britain's defences? (The answer to all that bullshit was nothing; she wouldn't know a tank from a battleship)

When Profumo was asked about this in Parliament, he said he had not slept with her. His lies were found out and he had to resign. As a result the whole Government collapsed.

I recall one of Stephen's interesting anecdotes that has stayed with me over the years. He told me he knew Ruth Ellis, the last woman to be hanged for murder, around six years previously in 1955. He claimed that there were others involved who were the real guilty parties.

Apparently, Stephen was in what was known as a *gentleman's club* later on the same day as Ruth had been sentenced to death. Here he saw the judge and the council for the prosecution having a drink and laughing about the verdict.

As he told me this he shuddered and said 'the establishment judiciary are truly evil, believe me'.

I still do believe him because the authorities are keeping the files on the Ruth Ellis case closed from public view until 2031. What are they hiding?

Sadly, Stephen himself would soon be trapped by those same evil forces, wheels were moving within wheels. The police and MI5 were looking for a fall guy, and Stephen was perfect for the roll of evil pimp because he put Chris up; so wasn't she living with him? They were both arrested; she went to prison on some trumped up charge and he was charged with living off immoral earnings! He may have had a weakness for pretty young women (well we all have our problems), but he was never a pimp and he didn't need to live off anyone. Indeed, he was very successful at what he did, and I would think very well off. How else could he afford handmade clothes in Mayfair, as well as live there and run a classic Jaguar car?

He was put on trial and was front-page news for weeks. The poor man must have gone through hell. He knew the powers that be were out to get him and that the verdict would be *'guilty'*. He knew too much about too many of the people who ran and controlled the Nation, Royalty

I tried desperately to think of a way out.

'This looks nice,' said Paula, as we entered a busy restaurant.

She was chatting away to me, but I couldn't take in what she was saying: I was too busy trying to compose myself.

No chance. I was already sweating like I was in the tropics.

With shaking hands I loosened my tie as the food arrived. I looked at my soup plate knowing that my hand was shaking so much I'd never get the spoon to my mouth without spilling it all over the table.

Just for good measure, I was now blushing a deep beetroot red.

The sounds going on around me – such as waiters calling out orders, other diners talking, background music – all began to blur into a mass of confusion in my head.

I felt sick with fear. If only I could just pass out, or even die.

It felt like everyone in the crowded place was staring at me.

Paula, definitely, had a look of puzzled horror. 'Steve, are you ill?' she asked.

The *SP* actor in me kicked in.

'Yes. I think I'm having a heart attack,' I lied. 'Please get me out of here.'

And she did, bless her.

Back at my place she insisted on calling a doctor who, of course, could find nothing wrong.

A couple of days' later I decided it was truth time. So, sitting quietly, having a coffee, I told her all about my nervous illness that we now know as *SP*.

She looked blank for a second or so, then said, 'you can't be serious. You don't expect me to believe that rubbish, do you? Look, if you have heart trouble or diabetes or epilepsy ... I love you and we can work it out together, but don't tell me silly lies. OK?'

So that, folks, was pretty much the end of it.

My next romance was with Tina. She was 30. Maybe I was thinking that an older woman who was now divorced, and had known good and bad times, would be more understanding. Wrong!

It all went well, but I carefully avoided social occasions, and she made that easy because she wasn't keen on parties and found going dancing a drag.

afflictions – they learn to live with them and often bravely overcome them – but the illogical and paralysing fear of phobias can bring you to a dead stop, no matter how much the reason for overcoming it means to you.

The force of the phobia can be insurmountable. And the damage it can cause a life is devastating and far-reaching.

What I'm about to relate to you will prove just that.

As I passed the American Embassy, I noticed a young woman taking photos of the building. Nothing unusual in that; tourists did it all the time. Today, you'd risk getting shot by security guards, but the Sixties were a much less violent and much more innocent time.

As I drew level with her, she moved back to get a better picture and stepped on my foot, then spun round and gripped my arm, saying, 'Hey, I'm real sorry. Did I hurt you?'

Her accent was unmistakably American, with a slight western drawl. The face was not classically beautiful, but quirky and pretty; the hair, shoulder-length and blonde; her figure, slim and petite; and, to top it all off, she had blue eyes and a dazzling smile.

Take it from me: love at first sight is a fact because from that second on I was hooked.

'No, I'm fine. I can limp to the nearest hospital to get my broken toes fixed,' I replied, trying to keep a straight face.

We stood there chatting and laughing like old friends. I felt cool and relaxed. Could I be the same person who, an hour ago, had been suffering the hellish torment of *SP*?

Within fifteen minutes I knew her life story – well, so far, that is.

Her name was Kate. She had been over here two months; loved London; rented a small furnished flat in Earls Court; and worked in an office nearby.

Back home, her "Mom" was "real sick", so she would be going home soon to see her, but would then return to London where she intended staying for a long time.

Even today, I could take you to the exact place in the square where we met.

The whole thing seemed surreal to me; it was nothing short of pure magic.

She mentioned that Trafalgar Square was next on her list for taking more photos to send to her friends back home, and asked if I could direct her.

'I can, but it's too far to walk. You'll have to take a cab.'

'Are you real busy right now?' she asked, turning on that

hope she's right.

We saw each other almost every night from then on, doing everything and nothing; window-shopping in Oxford Street; going to movies and at least one evening a week going to Freddie's club.

One Saturday, I remember, we went on the open top tourist bus, seeing all the famous landmarks in London. The weather was warm and sunny. Kate took about a dozen rolls of film. I'd seen all the places before, but they appeared different because she was with me.

One night, she stayed over at my place and we made love. It was relaxed and beautiful. I can only describe it as beyond anything.

And so this love affair continued on its way. We were just happy in each other's company.

Most nights she was at my place; sometimes I would go to hers. She loved the movies, so we'd take in a film at least once a week; and at weekends went sightseeing, places such as St Paul's Cathedral and the Tower of London, and did trips on the river.

She had a very independent streak and always wanted to pay her share. Nice in a way, I suppose, but I found it slightly annoying.

By careful planning, and a great deal of luck during these weeks, I managed to avoid any situation that would throw me into the depths of *SP* in front of her.

My brief explanation about having a breakdown and nervous trouble had only skimmed the surface of my real problem. I had still not been able to sit down and tell her in detail about my *SP*; I just kept putting it off. It never seemed to be the right time; I was just so terrified of rocking this wonderful boat.

I was to pay dearly for such delay.

One evening, when Kate was lying on my floor reading a magazine, she looked up, yawned, stretched, and said, 'Hey, I forgot to tell you. One of our directors is leaving tomorrow. He's been at the firm like about two hundred years, and they are giving a little farewell party for him, so come on over, have a drink or two, meet some of my work pals. They might even go to the expense of laying on music, so we can have a dance. It'll only last a couple of hours, then we can come back here.'

My heart sank. What could I say to such a casual request that held so much menace for me? I heard myself say, 'Sure. About what time?'

'Oh, say around six.'

I knew I was trapped.

The next day, just before a quarter to six, I was dressed and ready; looking good, but feeling like hell on earth.

From my flat to her office was less than a mile, so I began a slow walk, hoping that breathing deep lungfuls of evening air would steady my nerves.

As I turned the corner into Duke Street, I could see the lights were on in her first floor office; the windows were open, and I could hear the sound of people talking and laughing; in the background, pop music was playing.

The main door to the building was open, and next to the entrance hung a metal plate with the name of each firm on the four floors. A paper card had been stuck next to one of the names, saying, 'If you're a guest of Doring & Co's party, come right up...and welcome.'

It was then that the nightmare hit me with force.

Within seconds, mild nerves turned to stark, paralyzing fear. Every bit of strength left my body. In an instant, I became as weak as a kitten. One after another, the usual symptoms crept over me like I was being pulled under by a giant wave of panic. I felt consumed by a total loss of control. I've never jumped from a plane, so I don't know, but it must be like a parachutist would feel falling through the sky, frantically pulling the ripcord, knowing he or she is doomed because the parachute won't open.

I was now shaking and sweating, like someone with a high fever; a mouth so dry, I couldn't swallow. My mind was in such conflict. I felt utterly bewildered.

I stood at the foot of those stairs, engulfed in a nightmare.

I wanted more than anything to go up to the party where Kate was waiting for me; to meet her friends, have a drink, chat to people – the sort of things most people would do without a second thought.

Yet here I was, holding on to the banister rail so tight that my knuckles had gone white; my foot on the first stair, unable to move up to the next one. And if I did make it to the top, what the hell would Kate do when she saw me like this?

I could hear her voice from the night before, saying, 'I want to show you off to my girlfriends.'

Looking and acting like this, she wouldn't! I'd be a total embarrassment and show her up. She'd almost certainly dump me. No way could I risk it.

I know I'd warned her slightly by saying I had some nervous trouble, but nothing could prepare her for this.

I was now so disorientated that I stumbled out of the hallway, feeling my way along the wall like a blind man trying to get out of a burning building.

I retreated to a dark doorway across the street, and hid in the shadows, my heart still beating so fast that I could hear it inside my head. I crouched there, gasping for breath, trying desperately to get back in control. It was like being under the spell of some demonic force of evil.

I knew my entire future and the chance of happiness were at stake; absolutely nothing was more important to me than attending this small social occasion. All I had to do was cross the street and climb a few stairs. Kate would greet me; I'd shake a few hands; make small talk; have a sherry or two.

'Now come on, Steve, you can do it,' I told myself out loud, but this demonic force sent a reply to my brain saying, 'No, not quite. If you're a social phobic there is no way you'll do it, so don't even try.'

'But I *must* try. I *must.*'

I moved out of the doorway and looked up again at the office windows. The music was louder now. The party was starting to swing.

Then I caught sight of Kate, wearing a red dress. She leaned out and looked up the street in the direction from where I would approach.

I stepped back quickly into the shadows, instinctively knowing I'd lost the battle – and maybe even the war.

How I got through the next day at work, I'll never know.

As soon as I turned my key in the door that night, my phone started ringing. It was my beloved Kate.

'Hi there.' That now familiar greeting before starting a conversation. 'Why did you stand me up at the party? I bet you took a better-looking dame to some fancy night spot.'

'Kate,' I said, 'be serious for a moment. I love you and want to marry you. As for the party, I wanted to be there more than you could possibly know. Something beyond my control prevented me. I'll come over and explain. I should have done so before now.'

'Hold on, my darling future husband,' she replied with a laugh in her voice, 'it's no big deal. The party was slow, anyway. I looked out for you a couple of times, and left early and phoned to see if you were OK, but got no reply.'

No, I thought to myself, *because I was walking back from the same party.*

'Steve, darling, tell me something.' The tone of her voice was lower, more thoughtful. 'When we marry, if I ever got homesick, would you at some future time consider moving stateside?'

'To be with you, Kate, I'd live at the North Pole. Yes, of course I would. I like the American way of life.'

'Gee, that's great. Now, Steve, I've had some bad news. A neighbour phoned to say Mom is in hospital. She's had another heart attack, so I must stay by the phone all through tonight because it's daytime back home.'

'Kate, I'm so sorry to hear this. I'll come over to keep you company.'

'No. I've told my firm I won't be in, but you have to work tomorrow. I'll be round to meet you from work. OK?'

So that's how we left it.

As I walked out of my firm the next day...no Kate.

I dashed to my flat, thinking she'd be there, but no.

I'd been in about ten minutes when I saw a note lying on the doormat; I must have stepped over it.

Steve, darling, Mom's in a coma. I'm leaving for the airport right now. Will keep in touch every day. Pray for her. L.A, Kate. ("L.A" was our secret code for "Love Always".)

I must point out, my reader friend, this was before the days of emails, mobile phones, answering machines; back then, people wrote notes to each other all the time.

Nothing happened for more than a week. I tried to keep calm, but inside I was screaming.

Every day, I'd pick up the receiver on my phone to make sure it was working.

Then a large airmail postcard arrived. I've kept it all these years, along with our Trafalgar Square photo. It's in front of me now. It reads:*Steve, darling. Arrived back in USA safely. Phoned hospital. Mom's not going to make it. Hope I'm in time to say goodbye. I have an hour's wait for my Greyhound bus connection, then a two-hour ride. Would you consider flying out to help me thru this? Then we could return to London together. I need you. Will phone as soon as I get home. L.A, Kate xxx.*

The card had an N.M. postmark (New Mexico), but it had been posted a week before.

'I need you, too, my Kate, so why in God's name haven't

you phoned since then?' I said aloud, then I sat on the settee sobbing uncontrollably.

I checked with the people at her firm who were helpful, but as mystified as I was – they'd heard nothing.

A month later, I arranged to meet Kate's landlord at her flat. He lived further down the road. He was a very old Asian guy, one of life's gentlemen. I knew he sensed my desperation as he let me into Kate's flat.

The first thing to hit me was the slight smell of her perfume still lingering in the air; her clothes were hanging in the wardrobe; her books and records were everywhere. Everything I touched or looked at brought back memories of so much happiness.

The photo of the two of us was in a small frame beside her bed.

I asked the old man if I could take it.

'Yes, of course you can,' was his reply. Then he added, 'She did intend to return, you know, because her rent is paid for the next six weeks.'

I gave him my name and address, and asked that if he heard anything would he please let me know.

He placed his hand on my shoulder, and said, 'I give

you my solemn promise that I will.'

A couple of months later, I received a letter from him enclosing a cheque for £100 and saying: 'This is the deposit your young lady paid when she took on the flat. I'm sending it to you because you're the only person I know connected with her. I regret to tell you that I have not heard anything from her and no-one has called at the flat. We have an old saying in my country that may help you at this time. It translates like this: "Never seek the wind in the field. It is useless to try and find what is gone."'

I never heard from Kate again.

If only I had asked for her home address. For years after, the pain in my heart was so bad that it was almost physical.

Over the years I've had a million theories about what might have happened – that would take too long to go into here – but what I do know for absolute certain is that the real killer was severe *SP*.

If I had been able to attend that small office party, I would have been with Kate when she got the bad news from home and, most likely, would have flown out there with her.

My life would have taken off in such a different direction

once I had confided in Kate completely about *SP*. I would, with her help and love, have overcome it very quickly.

I knew it then. I know it now.

My Descent Into Isolation

It was, of course, inevitable that Cyril my boss would want a word with me about my strange behaviour. He was a decent and fair man, but he had a business to run.

As we sat in his office he looked baffled as he asked, 'what's wrong, Steve?'

I gave him a truthful answer. I explained all about *SP* and ended by saying, 'Cyril, I think I'm going mad.'

His reply was straight to the point.

'Rubbish. You're intelligent and quite sane, but you could be having a nervous breakdown. Take two weeks off with pay. Go right away somewhere for a complete break. Get away from it all. Come back refreshed and relaxed.'

I took his advice, slung a few things in a bag, got in the car and drove right the way down to St Tropez in the south of France.

The weather was fantastic. I swam in the sea every day, got a great suntan, and looked fit.

How does that old saying go? 'You take yourself wherever you go.'

Very true. When it came to having dinner in the hotel dining room, I froze with fear again as the waiter showed me to my table. I wondered if soldiers in the trenches of the First World War had felt as scared as I did right then.

I sat staring down at the tablecloth so as not to catch the eye of the other guests at the tables around me.

The fear was too much to cope with. I literally ran out of the dining room before any food arrived.

Back in my hotel room I felt humiliated, desperate and stupid.

From then on, I had all my meals in my room.

On my return to London I told Cyril I could no longer do the job I loved, and sadly handed in my notice and said my goodbyes. I regret to say that I never worked in the fashion industry again.

I sold the car, gave up the expensive flat and moved to New Cross, a poor, rundown suburb in southeast London. There I rented a very small, very cheap flat.

I went there because I had grown up nearby and so knew the area, and I had a sister living a couple of miles away in Lewisham. She was no help at all because she could never get her head around *SP*, and her husband was moving up fast in the law firm he worked for and was about to be offered a partnership. So they made it clear there was no room in their upper class legal lives for phobics, social or otherwise.

I was now out of work and living on the small amount of money that I had saved.

I'd spend long, lonely hours in my room reading medical books that I'd borrowed from the library about mental illness; these books described people who were very unbalanced, and, in many cases, dangerous to themselves and others.

Rightly or wrongly, I had always thought of myself as having a nervous illness (not a mental one). I was, I believed, perfectly sane and normal except for this one strange, paralysing and devastating nervous illness.

Knowing I would soon run out of money, I signed on at the unemployment office where you got paid by the government a very small amount each week, barely enough for one meal a day; but, understandably, they do insist you try and find work, and, if after a few weeks you don't start work, they stop the money.

I wanted to work but couldn't find a job suitable for a social phobic. How could I be a shop assistant, salesman or demonstrator in a department store or, in fact, do anything that involved mixing with people?

As the illness progressed, I started to feel safer at night.

I know it sounds strange (come to that, I guess my whole story does), but getting on an empty bus at night was not as frightening as getting on a crowded one during the day.

So I found night work at a factory. I started work at 10pm and finished at 6am. As trucks pulled into the loading bay, five of us had to unload them – and fast; it was hard, heavy work.

I was only taken on for three nights a week, so the pay was lousy. I was now around thirty, so maybe they thought I was a bit too old for it. They were right: a full five or six days would have killed me.

The guys I worked with were a good crowd, but I couldn't mix.

I'd take a sandwich to have at break time and eat it sitting in the back of one of the trucks.

I could never face going to the canteen. I tried just once, got as far as putting my hand on the door handle to go in, then I heard the sound of all the workers talking and laughing. I pushed the door open about six inches, and saw that I'd have to walk past rows of tables full of men and women to get to the counter and order what I wanted; then I would have to carry my tray back to my table and sit with a crowd of people and talk with those next to me. You may as well have asked me to swim the Atlantic ... impossible.

So, I headed back to the safety of the cold, empty truck.

I was now finding it very hard to make ends meet.

I had long since sold all my expensive clothes. The lumber jacket and trousers I owned I had bought second-hand from charity shops; the same with my shoes and shirts.

Of course, I had no car, phone, TV, nor even a cooker; just a small microwave and one electric fire.

Then I moved to an even smaller flat near the river in Greenwich.

This one was a bed-sit: that's just one room with a bathroom and toilet down the hall that you have to share with the other tenants in the block. But it was all I could afford.

For my one small, but decent, meal every day, I went to a Church Army hostel about a mile away.

The Church Army is a great organisation, a bit like the Salvation Army. It helps those who are very poor or down and out, and provides a hot meal for them, rather like a soup kitchen.

The other diners were an assorted group of tramps, winos and drifters. They all seemed lost in their own private hell, so there was not much need to make conversation.

Unloading trucks at night was nearly killing me, so I found another night job, this time cleaning public toilets.

There were four of us who would travel by van and visit six public toilets each night around the Central London area. I'll spare you the very unpleasant details, but it could at times be the most filthy and disgusting work; I had to develop a strong stomach.

We would move in looking like a hit squad from outer space, covered from head to foot in protective clothing, and carrying our hoses and brushes, but, as I was living in the unreal world of *SP*, it suited me because the hours were midnight until 5am with no breaks. So, no panic about having to face a canteen and, once I had on my spacesuit, no one could see if I was trembling or blushing. Most important of all, it paid the rent.

I did, of course, realise only too well how low I'd sunk and felt, as always, desperate.

Finally, I decided to seek medical advice. I'd not done so since Stephen Ward had tried to help me, I kept hoping I would somehow be able to pull myself together or shake it off.

Over the years I had fallen into a way of life where I kept away as best I could from any situation that brought on *SP*, but it had now got to the stage where almost all situations would do just that.

My local doctor appeared not to be paying any attention as I explained my embarrassing symptoms; he muttered something about it being a mental problem.

Then, looking up from his endless writing, he said, 'Do you ever think you're someone important?'

'Like who?' I asked.

'Well, like a king or a billionaire or maybe a famous person from history.'

'No,' I replied wearily. 'No, I never think anything like that.'

Returning once more to his writing he added, 'I am sending you to the department of psychiatry and neurology at Lewisham hospital. You will see the head consultant, a Mr. Norton. He's a top man, and will have you right in no time. Goodbye.' He said it with an air of finality; in other words: 'Piss off. You've had your three minutes of my valuable time.'

Well, if his idea of 'in no time' was another forty years of hell, then I suppose his estimate was spot-on.

About a month later I got an appointment for the hospital.

By the time the big day arrived, I had rehearsed over and over all that I was going to tell the consultant. Nothing was to be held back; he would hear the whole dreadful story of how *SP* had just about destroyed me. And, please God, could he offer me some help at last?

After two secretaries had checked me out, and then double-checked me, a timid little nurse tapped very quietly on the great man's door.

'Enter,' said a reedy, high-pitched voice.

A small man with a shiny bald head was sitting behind an enormous desk, writing furiously as if he had some impossible deadline to meet.

'Sit there,' he snapped, pointing with his pen to a hard uncomfortable-looking chair.

At last he put his pen down and said, 'I have read your doctor's notes, and all these situations that worry you concern other people.'

'They don't worry me,' I said. 'They cripple me with absolute fear.'

'Yes. You're suffering with people phobia,' he replied. Then he began writing again.

These medical types must write the equivalent of the entire works of William Shakespeare every week! Today, of course, their writing pads have given way to computers, so now, to avoid eye contact, they stare at a monitor as they tell you that you're ill.

Could it be that the medical profession has patient phobia?

He wrote out a prescription for drugs, handed it to me and said, 'Get these, and start taking them at once.'

"Timid Nurse" must have been listening at the keyhole, because just as I got up to leave she opened the door from the other side.

So, less than thirty minutes after entering the hospital, I was back on the street.

The next morning I took the first two tablets, hoping for a miracle.

I ventured out onto the busy streets, thinking I might try the local shops to get some tinned food that I was running low on, instead of going to my usual 24-hour supermarket where I would shop at around 5am when the place was deserted.

My head trembling was now so bad that I looked forward to the winter, when I could wear my coat collar up all the time. Other people did that to protect them from the cold wind; I did it to hide my shaking.

Like a fool, I thought these drugs would wave a magic wand for me and I would be able to walk past bus queues with my head held high, instead of my usual way of staring intently at the pavement to avoid all eye contact. Hey, I might even get talking to someone; engage in some casual conversation.

I guess I got over-excited, elated even, because at last I was fighting back, doing something positive about *SP* with the help of the medical world. I was about to get my life back.

But I was about to learn one of life's very sad lessons.

The effects of the drug kicked in, less than half an hour after I'd left my flat.

I began to shake violently in short bursts – not the usual *SP* shaking; this was more like convulsions, like I was having a fit.

My vision became blurred and my legs gave way. I staggered as far as a seat outside a shop where I collapsed.

I knew I couldn't make it home, so I just sat there for I don't know how long, maybe an hour, when a man and a woman asked me if I was ill and did I need help.

I tried to explain, but my speech was too slurred; my mouth and entire face had gone numb: there was no feeling.

Thank God for those two angels who got me into their car and took me back to the flat.

I've no idea who they were, but I was really lucky that they had come my way that day, bless 'em.

I passed out on my settee for the rest of the day, and was finally woken by my neighbour's cat, which had got in through the window and was licking my face.

To my horror I realised I'd soiled my trousers during this ordeal, so spent the evening washing and cleaning up.

I felt too ill to go to work that night, so London's public toilets stayed dirty and unattended.

The only medication I had taken before this had been an aspirin for a headache. Could that be the reason why the drugs had had such an awful reaction on me? Or, much more likely, had Norton given me medication that was totally unsuitable and far too strong?

My own fault for expecting too much, but I was just so very disappointed.

At my second meeting with him he seemed unconcerned when I told him about my passing out in the street due to the drugs he'd given me.

Pushing his chair back and putting his hands behind his head he began asking questions ... so the rest of our meeting was taken up with sex. Not, I hasten to add, between Norton and me, but with his probing into every detail of my non-existent sex life. The man appeared to be totally obsessed with the subject.

When I was a child, was I attracted to any of my male schoolteachers? He asked, with great interest.

'No,' I told him, 'I wasn't. In my mind's eye, I can recall ugly old Mr. Henshaw of Class 3. I had my doubts if Mrs. Henshaw could stand the sight of him.'

'Did you want to put your hand in his trousers and play with his balls?' asked Norton.

'No, never,' I replied again, 'but I did long to get out into the playground and play football.'

'When did you last expose yourself in public?' he continued.

'I never have, and what's more I've no wish to do so.'

I'd just about had enough. I'd expected so much and I was getting this crap, so I went on, 'But last week I did piss myself in public, thanks to you and the dangerous drugs you gave me. You're a very highly paid, twisted, compassionless bastard.'

"Timid Nurse" almost passed out, Norton gasped for air like a fish on dry land and I was back on the street again. And I must admit, I felt better than I had done in ages.

It didn't last, of course.

A few days later I had ventured out during daylight hours because I had to go to the post office to collect a small amount of money owed to me by the unemployment office.

The clerk pushed a form across the counter. 'Sign there, please,' he said, handing me his pen, 'and also fill in your name and address.'

SP came to the surface at once, my hand began to shake uncontrollably and a feeling of intense fear took me over. I bluffed my way out by saying, 'Damn. I've left my reading glasses in the car. I won't be a minute.'

With that, I fled out the door. I could feel his suspicious look, and that of other people who had been standing nearby, boring into my back.

Of course, there was no car or glasses. Once outside, I lent against the wall, trying to regain control. Then I filled in the form, returned to the post office and got my money. But those what I call "nasty turns" happened to me on a daily basis.

The years were passing, as they do. I was nearly forty, but the mirror told me I looked more like I was in my mid-fifties.

I had given up my career in public toilet cleaning when they cut back on the wages and increased the hours.

Over the years I tried more jobs than I care to remember: night work in dozens of factories; I drove a van for the school meals service; I delivered motor parts. For a year I worked as a night security guard, walking endless corridors in huge government buildings, checking countless doors and windows. It was fine because I worked alone, never having to speak to anyone, or deal with any type of mixing with people, or be seen.

Then they told me I had to change to the day shift. During the day those same buildings would be swarming with people. I'd be the uniformed guard standing in the busy foyer; people would approach me asking directions; I'd be up front, on show, having to deal with anything and everything.

There was, of course, no way I could handle that, so I was unemployed again. And my age was starting to tell against me. Even for the poorly paid night work that I sought, they really wanted men in there twenties.

About this time I noticed I never felt well. As if *SP* wasn't enough to deal with, I always felt slightly sick and had a raw pain in my stomach.

There was a large park near my flat that had great views looking out over London and the River Thames. When the pain got bad I'd go there and sit for a couple of hours, enjoying the fresh air before getting ready to start work at night.

One day at the park, the pain came on so bad that I passed out and fell on the ground where I stayed for some time. The first person to pass by went through my pockets and stole my wallet that contained the huge sum of £4. The next person to find me was kind enough to call an ambulance that took me to Bromley hospital.

When I came to, some days later in the intensive care ward, the surgeon asked me how long I'd had a large duodenal ulcer. I told him it was news to me.

'Well, you had a very bad one.'

'What do you mean, I "had one"?'

'Well, you see, we had to operate. You were haemorrhaging: that is, passing blood. You'd lost a great amount by the time you arrived here. I had to remove about a third of your stomach. You will be with us for some time because you're also suffering from malnutrition, so we are going to keep a close eye on you. You had no identification on you and, being so poorly dressed, we assumed you were a tramp. But the police tell us you had been robbed while you were unconscious. Tell the nurse who you want us to contact and we will phone them at once.'

The awful truth dawned on me that there was no one.

Here I was, fighting for my life in hospital after having had major surgery and the hospital staff had assumed I was a tramp, and all because I had spent the last twenty five years avoiding people that I couldn't face, only venturing out to work at night in low-down, low-pay jobs where you never made friends. The staff had noticed how poorly dressed I was; there was a time when all my clothes were handmade and of the finest materials. This, I knew in my heart, was all down to *SP*; this strange life-altering illness had brought me to this. At one time I'd had it all, but *SP* takes it all away and you're left with nothing.

Mr. Scott, the surgeon, shook my hand when I left the hospital after a six-week stay and told me to take it very easy.

'You're almost six feet tall, but you weigh under nine stone. You must build yourself up. Eat the best food,' he said. He was a good man and meant well, so I didn't bother to explain that good food was expensive and I couldn't afford it.

On entering my old flat, I was stunned to see that most of my furniture had been stolen in my absence. The thieves had smashed the window to get in. Who would want such old rubbish was a mystery: maybe they wanted to start a bonfire.

I spent most of my time reading medical books that "Catman" (that's the name I gave my neighbour down the hall because he had three of them) got for me at the library – I couldn't face going there myself.

So, after all these years, I was still trying to find an answer to it all.

I read about psychiatry, psychoanalysis, psychosis and psychology, and every other "-ology" you can think of, but these books had no answer for me.

I seriously began to think I was the only person in the world who suffered from this strange and terrifying condition.

I was still too weak to work, and some days felt so ill that I stayed in bed all day. But I needed money, or I'd be out of the flat and with no roof over my head.

I saw a job advertised in the paper for cleaners. They wanted people to clean railway carriages at night at Charing Cross station. That's an end-of-the-line main line station in the heart of London. It was only four stops down the line from my local station, and the cleaning company would pay the travelling costs.

I went out to a phone box and called the company. *SP* never affected me when using the phone; I didn't like using it, but I could do it. I never stuttered, I never dried up, blushed, trembled, nor generally lost the plot, like I did in all other situations.

The girl I spoke with asked a few questions about me, and I lied by knocking 12 years off my age and saying I was very fit and used to hard work. She asked if night work worried me. I told her the truth, saying I preferred it, but I did not mention why ... hardly the time to get into a conversation about *SP*. She told me to be at the station the next night to start work and to wear old clothes.

'You get half an hour's break. There is no canteen, so bring a sandwich.'

Really sounds great, I thought, but by now I was used to being treated like crap by employers. When you reach the bottom of the pile you get kicked around.

The next night I was at the station, along with a small crowd of other cleaners. I was given a mop, a broom and a pail of soapy water, and assigned to one of the empty carriages that were parked up in a long line for the night; they moved out again at 5am. In that time I had to do three: that's clean the seats, floors, windows, doors. It was hard and boring, the train's heating was off and, being winter, it was very cold. I never spoke with anyone, never had to face anyone, and, when the shift was over, I headed home and was back at the flat by 7am where I could hide from the world for the rest of the day.

When I look back on my life at that time I realise that it wasn't a life at all, not even an existence. The tragedy was that I now, after so many years, accepted it as normal.

One early morning, as I sat on the platform waiting for my train home, a fireman walked towards me, smiling.

'So, you never became world champion?' he asked, with a big friendly grin.

Then it dawned on me. It was Dave Mason, an old school pal. We had been in the ring together at the old boxing club. I'd not seen him since I was fourteen. He looked so smart in his uniform, and there was me dressed in my old cleaning overalls. He told me he had done twenty-two years in the fire service, so he was going to retire soon on a good pension. Then he and his wife intended going to live in Canada, where he had a married son. He also had two married daughters and a year-old granddaughter.

We reminisced about old friends and places, then he said, 'I saw you once, when we were in our twenties. You were walking along Oxford Street. You looked the business, real smart. I couldn't stop to speak, I was in a car, but I remembered you went into the tailoring fashion world.'

There was an awkward silence, like he wanted to say: 'What the hell happened?'

So I said, 'Yes, I was in that trade long ago. Since then, I've had a lot of ill health: stomach ulcers, operations, you name it.'

Of course, I didn't mention the real problem – *SP*.

'Did you ever marry?' he asked.

'No. Never found "Miss Right",' was the silly reply I gave.

Just then, his train pulled in on the other platform. He jumped to his feet and, holding out his hand, said, 'You take care, old friend.'

'And you, Dave. Good luck in Canada.'

He walked away, then turned and came back, saying, 'That last fight we had. I won on points, didn't I?'

'No, by a knockout,' I told him.

'Right. So don't argue with me or I'll do it again.' He said it with a huge smile, then pushed a £20 note into my top pocket, and jumped on his train as it pulled out.

I got to my feet and waved to him. He waved back as the train disappeared from view. I hope he didn't see the tears in my eyes.

Back at the flat, I felt even more depressed than usual. I kept thinking about Dave and how good his life had been, and how lousy mine was in comparison and it was all down to *SP*.

Even on the way home from work, I wanted to buy some tea at the corner shop and change the £20 note that Dave had kindly given me, but there were about five or six people in there. Just standing at the door, I felt scared. I knew when I got to the counter I'd freeze up and not be able to get the words out, and I'd blush and tremble. So I decided to leave it until later that evening when it might be empty.

What a way to live, constantly anxious, worried and depressed.

It follows that anyone with *SP* must suffer depression, and I'd been depressed for many years now.

If you don't suffer the hell of depression, it's impossible to explain to you how vile and awful it is. You don't think you can go on living any more. You have an appalling sense of despair and absolutely no hope that things will ever get better.

My doctor had put me on anti-depressants years before that. I still took them each day, but they seemed to have little, if any, effect.

He had also referred me to a counsellor. Just like Norton, she seemed obsessed with my past sex life and had a mania for writing while I spoke to her, so, after about three visits, I stopped going.

Over the past twenty years I had also tried hypnotherapy, homeopathy and faith healing, but nothing had worked. I just became more worried about my *SP* and reached the very depths of unhappiness.

I don't know why, but that day I looked through my old photo album. There was Mum and Dad; they had both died many years before.

I thought, *If only they were here now to talk to*, but then, if they were, it would still be hard work making conversation with them; they could never open up and speak from the heart. Couldn't they see how unhappy their teenage son was?

Looking more closely at the photo, I could see once more how miserable they were with each other, so how could they help anyone else? It occurred to me that I never saw them share a laugh or a joke. They were decent enough people in their way, but I cursed them for bringing me into this world that I knew I now had to find the courage to leave.

I sat in my one armchair with a cup of tea in my hand for hours. As the day wore on it got dark, and I continued sitting there with the light off.

It's very strange, the odd things that come into your mind at such a time.

I recalled years before visiting the family of another short-lived romance: this girl was real keen to show me off to her parents. The meeting was going fairly well until her father asked me to pour out some wine. I can still see the four empty glasses on the table. As I lifted the bottle, my hand began to shake violently; some of the wine went in the glasses, but most went all over the floor. The silence was deafening. Then her father said quietly, 'you need to get a grip of your nerves, son.'

I replied, 'If I were in this room alone, my hand would be as steady as a rock.'

'I know it would,' he said.

The two women said nothing.

I often wished I'd got to know that man better. I sensed that he understood *SP*, but I never did. I just picked up my coat and left.

Later, I received a letter from the girl saying, 'Let's call it a day for now, but do get back in touch when you get over your nervous trouble'.

Would she have said that if I had suffered an asthma attack?

People are not sympathetic towards *SP* sufferers because we embarrass them by our actions. Collapse on the floor, fight for your breath – they can handle it. Blush, tremble, shake and stutter, and you're on your own.

As the night wore on, I calmly decided that enough was enough.

I looked at Dave's £20 note and thought that I should post it back to him, but I had no idea where he lived.

It dawned on me that I had nothing to leave anyone and there was no point in a suicide note – who would I address it to, and who would read it?

SP had finally destroyed me.

Fighting it every day for years, with no help from anywhere, had totally exhausted me. I reasoned that handfuls of aspirins mixed with sleeping tablets would put me to sleep forever.

The human mind is, indeed, mysterious. Here I was, calmly getting ready to kill myself, one of the most horrendous things anyone can do. Yet if you had asked me to attend a pleasant social occasion that evening instead, I would have been petrified.

I took 10 tablets straight off with a mouthful of tea, then looked once more through the old photos, thinking that the answer lay in the long-distant past.

It occurred to me that all the photos of me showed an unhappy looking child. The problem with that theory is that many people have an unhappy start in life, but they don't develop *SP*.

So, even as I started to feel drowsy and drifted towards death, I was still to be denied an answer to the question: Why me; why *SP*?

I suppose I was hoping for a last-minute reprieve in the form of knowing the reason for this destructive affliction, but it was not to be.

And, my friend, I have to tell you that sadly I still, to this day, have never found a convincing, definite reason for its onset.

So I just sat there, taking three or four tablets at a time with my now cold tea. I thought about Kate, and somehow knew she had passed on and was waiting for me. I sensed she was in the room with me telling me she had died within days of returning home. I tried to get up and make a fresh cup of tea, but my legs felt like they were made of lead, and I fell back into my armchair.

One of the tablets broke up in my mouth; the bitter taste caught in my throat, sending me into a fit of coughing.

I was now lapsing in and out of consciousness.

When I came to again – I don't know if it was minutes or hours later – tears were streaming down my face. I had the strange sensation of being on the other side of the room, looking at myself as though watching an event taking place that had nothing to do with me.

My last sensation was of being, I thought, paralysed. I wanted to take more tablets, but couldn't move a muscle. I just sat motionless, staring at the silvery moon in the black sky outside my window. I was aware that the window was open about four inches at the bottom; I wondered if the cat down the hall would find me like he did last time.

They say the hearing is the last thing to shut down. It was with me. For what seemed a long time after my eyes closed, I could hear the traffic going by outside. It had been raining and the tires made a swishing sound on the road, but my last overriding emotion was that of loneliness and despair.

To this day, I'm sure in my own mind that, for some hours after becoming unconscious, I was in another dimension – not death itself, or I wouldn't be here now, but on the very edge of it – and it was very peaceful.

The cat from down the hall did not visit me that night, but his owner, "Catman", did. He came looking for it, thinking it was with me.

He told me later that he'd come to my room that night, but got no answer. So he'd called again early the next morning. This time he opened the door, and in the dawn light saw me in the chair, came over and said, 'Sorry to trouble you, Steve, but have you seen Snowy?' (Actually, his beloved cat had spent the night on the roof.) He then said out loud to himself, 'Oh, my God. He's dead.'

117

Lisa, Jack and So Many Others

The ambulance took me to Greenwich hospital where I was given the stomach pump treatment. This, in turn, caused my old ulcer scar to bleed again, so I was back in intensive care for a week, then on the general ward for another two weeks. They did a good job, medically speaking, but not from where I was standing. I wanted to be dead.

The surgeon, Mr Scott, who had done my previous operation, came to see me on the day I was leaving.

He sat in a chair beside the bed and started by saying, 'Y'know, all your illness and this suicide attempt is caused by extreme stress, so what is it in your life that could be that stressful? I'd like to know.'

I thought: *OK, you asked for it.*

I gave him the A to Z of *SP* and how I tried to exist with it, and I ended by saying, 'I don't suppose you've ever heard of it.'

'Yes indeed, I have,' he said quietly. 'And I think I can help. I shall make an appointment for you to go to the Maudsley psychiatric hospital over at Denmark Hill.'

I told him what a waste of time it had been going to Lewisham hospital so many years before and about my run-in with Norton.

'You will find,' he said, 'that during the last thirty or more years the treatment for your type of medical condition has changed completely. No one should be living the way you are, so give it a try. You'll be treated as an outpatient. They will probably give you group therapy twice a week for three hours at a time.'

I thanked him, but felt half-hearted about group therapy, or whatever it was, and dreaded going to the place.

It was only a short journey by bus from my place, but sheer hell for me waiting at the crowded bus stop during the day. Almost every time, someone would ask me what number bus they needed to get to some place. I would start to stutter and blush, and struggle to get the words out. Most times they would turn away and ask some other person in the queue, leaving me feeling crushed.

The class – if that's the right word – at the hospital was small. About thirty lost souls of both sexes and all ages.

The doctor was a pleasant, relaxed woman in her thirties. She introduced us all, one at a time, by our first names, then told us to shake hands with the person either side of us. She then read out a description of each individual's symptoms (most of them were severe *SP* in one form or another), then asked us to put our hands up when it was our case that she read out (but only if we wanted to), and then she wanted the rest of the class to give that sufferer a round of applause.

I must have felt brave that day because mine was the seventh one she read. I recognised it at once. So far, no one had owned up to his or her symptoms.

I put my hand up, thinking, *what the hell.* The class burst into applause. It felt good; it was like these people were saying, 'Well done, Steve. You did your best. We know what you've been through. Together we are going to make it. You're not on your own any more.'

Would you believe that, from then on, I began to look forward to my twice weekly visits.

I was no longer working because when I got back to the flat from hospital after my suicide attempt there was a letter waiting for me from the train cleaning company saying I'd been laid off. Just as well, because I was in far too weak a condition for that work.

So, I now had to exist on sickness benefit (a small payment paid by the government to those too ill to work).

The doctor had said that I must rest and try to put on weight.

I did try to do as he advised. If the weather was good, I'd go to the park and try and walk around it once, but I'd get so tired that halfway round would be enough.

Also, when in the park, I started to feel self-conscious. I was always alone, just walking along slowly. Everyone else was doing something: someone's kids were playing football; adults were playing tennis or walking their dogs. I tried saying 'Good morning' to those I saw every day, but never got a response. I was clean but poorly dressed, and, to be honest, I looked old and ill, so maybe that was the reason.

There was a small open air café that sold teas and ices, but my nerves wouldn't let me go up to the counter and order anything; to get there I would have to pass the few people sitting at the tables. I cursed myself, because I was often dying for a cup of tea.

At the hospital they'd put me on drugs that were supposed to help my *SP*. I would need an entire book – a big one – to list the names of all the various medications I tried. Some had no effect at all; others had a violent effect, with severe sickness and diarrhoea, or sent me into moods of deep depression, and some made me hyperactive.

I think mental confusion was the worst effect. I would stand for ages in the kitchen, trying to remember how to cut a slice of bread.

They would keep me on a particular drug for about three weeks, then try another one, and so it went on for close on two years.

The class therapy was the best for helping us. I recall one day the doctor said, 'We are all going to stand up, one at a time in front of the class, and say a few words.'

A deathly silence fell on the room, then a mass rush for the exit.

'Wait,' she called out, laughing. 'Come back and hear what I have to say. I want a volunteer, please. I need help.'

A big man got up and stood sheepishly at her side.

'OK. I want this man to have a round of applause.' He got it, long and loud.

She told us his name was Jack. He was an ex-soldier and looked like Burt Lancaster, the movie star. She put a reassuring arm around him and gave him a hug.

'Would any one of you like to thank Jack for coming up here?' she asked.

One at a time we got up and did so.

When I stood up, I said, 'Well done, Jack. I wish I could have gone out front like you just did.'

That meeting was the start of a great friendship.

Jack went on to say, in a quite nervous voice, 'I've not had *SP* for years like most of you people. It struck me down about two years ago and it's brought me to my knees. I can't go anywhere or do anything. It's destroyed my marriage, and my married daughter no longer keeps in touch. I lost my job. If I didn't have my army pension, I'd starve. This illness makes me feel stupid and desperate at the same time. What the hell can I do?'

A woman in the audience called out, 'You can get well like we all can. That's what we're here for.' This was greeted by more rapturous applause.

I turned to see an attractive young woman in her early twenties sitting a few rows behind me. She was well dressed and had an elegant air about her. I wondered what someone so poised was doing at a gathering of *SP* sufferers. I was to find out very soon.

The meeting was starting to take on a nice "all friends together" feeling. Several people got up and told how they suffered various forms of *SP*: how they blushed; stuttered; couldn't face a job interview or restaurant; always felt shy and awkward in the presence of others; could never mix, nor make friends.

One elderly man told us that for years he had read a passage from the bible in his church every Sunday, but could no longer stand up and face the congregation.

I was thinking to myself that the only reason any of us could stand up in front of this audience was because it was a totally sympathetic one. We knew we were talking to fellow sufferers.

I wasn't at all sure if it would work in real life; trying it in front of cold unhelpful outsiders who'd never heard of *SP*. We could find ourselves back at the hell of square one.

My thoughts were brought to a dead stop by someone shouting out, 'Bollocks. That's total shit.'

No-one said a word. The poor man out front quickly sat down. I turned to see the same elegant young woman holding her head in her hands in shame.

'I'm so sorry,' she said quietly.

The lady doctor took over, saying, 'Thank you, Lisa. Now listen everyone, let me explain. Lisa has *SP*, but this is brought on by her main illness called "Tourette's syndrome". As you can see, she blinks her eyes rather a lot. That is known as "nervous tics", but the hardest symptom she has to live with is that she has an uncontrollable urge to shout out swear words or meaningless rubbish in public.'

Lisa left her seat and came to the front. I thought for a moment she was going to shout more obscenities, but she simply said, 'Ask me anything you want.'

'What caused it?' asked Jack.

'I don't know, really. They tell me it's a brain abnormality.'

Another voice asked, 'Surely, when you feel you're going to shout out something, you can stop yourself, even if you just put your hand over your mouth?'

She gave a sad smile and said, 'Have you ever tried to suppress a sneeze?'

'What treatment are you being given?' asked another.

'I'm taking neuroleptic drugs.' The clinic tell me I may be on them the rest of my life.

She continued talking about her awful problem for some time.

Then I stood up and said, 'Can you imagine us two in a restaurant, me shaking so much I can't get the food to my mouth and you swearing at the top of your voice? I think it makes a very good case for eating at home.'

The whole room dissolved into laughter and we all needed that badly; there was, and had been, so little of it in our lives.

As time wore on, Jack and Lisa became my two best friends: in fact, my only friends.

After the class we would meet up in the park and discuss our progress – or lack of it.

Jack always had his puppy with him. I can't recall if his name was Bruno or Brutus, but Jack called him Bru, for short. He was a mixture of all the dogs you can name, but more Labrador than anything.

Lisa was an unmarried mum. She had a daughter, Lara, who was about three at the time, and she would bring her along too.

Jack, being the bravest, would go over to the café and get teas and sandwiches, and an ice cream for Lara, and would you believe I went with him to help bring it all back on a tray.

Lisa stayed at our table. 'In case I yell out something awful and get us all slung out.' She'd say it with a laugh, but we knew how hard it was for her.

I had never heard of her illness before. Thinking about it, I'd say it was as bad, if not worse, than *SP* in its crippling effect on one's life.

I remember Jack saying one sunny day, as we all sat looking out over the River Thames towards the City of London on the other side, 'One of my men lost both his legs when a shell burst near us while we were fighting during the war. If that had been me, I don't think it would have crippled me the way *SP* has.'

I started to say, 'You can't compare one situation with another, Jack...'

But he went on, 'I know because I keep in touch with the guy. He was one of my platoon. Sure, he's in a wheelchair and he's been through hell, but now he's getting on with his life. He laughs and jokes. And you know what? When he goes out in his chair people offer to help. When I paid for the teas just now and that little punk behind the counter handed me my change, I dropped it because of my hands shaking the way they do. And you know what? He laughed. I could have reached across the counter and punched him in the mouth.'

'Don't do that, Jack,' I said, 'because the kid wants another ice cream. I'd like another tea, and Bru has his eye on one of those sausage rolls.'

So we'd end up laughing.

Later, we took a walk around the Cutty Sark, that's a big old sailing ship that has been restored and is now in dry dock near the river. She's the last of the tea clippers, and back in the 1890s sailed from the UK to China and Australia.

We all had fun that day.

Sometimes we would all meet up at my flat. Lisa would go out for a takeaway – usually fish and chips – while I got the tea and coffee ready. Jack would go with her in case she shouted out something, as she often did.

Jack recalled that once, when she left the shop, she shouted at the top of her voice, 'Fuck London. I hate the place. Everyone should get out. There are no palm trees here.'

One of the customers called back; 'Why don't you go and live in Spain?' 'There are hundreds of palm trees over there'. All totally ridiculous of course, but tragic.

Jack's wife had left him and he now had a room in a rundown guest house in Blackheath. It was very hard for him to live alone after being used to his own place and family life. At least he still had transport: the old Ford that took him everywhere.

I couldn't afford one, but a car is a must for the *SP* sufferer. You're mobile without having to mix with others on public transport or even walking along the street.

It was a great treat for me when he took us all out. From the safety of the back seat I could look out on the passing world, and in broad daylight, too.

Apart from the park, we sometimes went to Lisa's place. She lived with her mother, Mary, who had a small house in

Catford. A charming lady who made us welcome. We would have a meal, and chat or watch the TV.

SP never bothered me there, I suppose, because everyone knew about it and the three of us had it. In fact, we hardly mentioned it. It was almost like being normal again, living like the rest of the world did.

Lisa's father had died young and she had a married sister who had two kids, but no other member of her family, past or present, had any sign of Tourette's syndrome.

Life went on this way for about a year, but the drugs they put me on one after another were getting to me. At times I was half out of my head, and not one of them made me feel better.

The therapy and role-playing did help, especially when we went out with the doctor onto the streets. We would go into busy supermarkets, pick a couple of items, then go through the checkout and pay for them while the rest of the class looked on. We were taken, on purpose, to very busy places.

The doctor said we all hid away from life because of our SP. Most of us only went out at night, so this was a real test for us.

One time we went to a very busy covered market and came to a stall selling clothing, and, guess what, Lisa's mum Mary was running it. She bought the whole crowd of us tea and coffee.

Lisa wasn't with us that day. Mary told us she never came to the market because if she started shouting and swearing she would never forgive herself for showing her mother up at her place of work. In fact, Lisa was turning up at the classes less and less.

Jack, too, seemed to be marking time, not really making any progress. He had tried to get work, but had been turned down for several jobs. There was a small, very quiet pub near his place, and, because I was feeling a fraction more confident, I'd meet him and, of course, his faithful Bru there and sit in the corner with a couple of beers. He missed so many things: his wife and daughter; and he missed army life. I noticed his hands were shaking worse than ever and he seemed very vague, like he was daydreaming. He told me if he didn't find work soon he'd have to sell the car.

'I've never been without a car since I was sixteen,' he said, like it was the end of the world. 'You know, Steve,' he went on, 'I should be at a reunion of my old regiment tonight, but I couldn't face it. I didn't want the lads to see me like this and I wouldn't be able to have a good old drink-up with them because of all these stupid drugs I'm on. By the way, did I tell you I had the electric treatment?' He said it almost as an after-thought.

'You did what, Jack? Say that again.'

'I had that ECT. I can't remember what it stands for.'

'It stands for *electro convulsive therapy*, and, if you weren't bigger, stronger and years younger than me, I'd knock you through that door. That's for those who are really severely depressed and at the end of the road.'

'Well, that's what I am, Steve. Look, I had it yesterday. Now, do you see any difference in me?'

He was like a brother to me; no way did I want to hurt him or see him hurt, so I lied.

'Yeah, you seem as nuts as ever.'

For the first time that night he smiled, and said, 'They give you an injection and, while you're asleep, they send an electric current through the brain that gives you a slight fit. Now I've got to have two of these a week for maybe eight or nine weeks.'

'No, Jack. You don't have to have anything. I don't like this "got to". Who the hell are these "got to" people? You're not in the army any more, Jack. You don't have to take orders.'

'Steve, these people are doctors.'

'For Christ's sake, Jack, the electric chair and the guillotine were invented by doctors.'

The barman, hearing our raised voices, gave a worried look in our direction.

'Steve, look, I am not responding to any of the drugs they're trying me on, and it's close on two years now. That therapy business; we stand up and talk to each other. We're preaching to the converted, pal. By now we should be able to give a speech at the Albert Hall to ten thousand people, but I still can't go into a café for a coffee. Nor can Lisa. She still shouts and swears at people in the street for no reason. You have improved slightly by the therapy class, but I have to repeat, pal, only slightly. Lisa and her Mum have an appointment to see one of the top doctors about her having that operation called "lobotomy". Lisa's heard that it really cuts down the anxiety you feel. You see, Steve, as nice and pleasant as it is, we can't spend the rest of our lives in the park.'

I held up my hand to stop him telling me any more.

'I can't believe I'm hearing this, Jack. Do you, or more importantly Lisa; know what that type of brain surgery entails? I assume they open up the skull to get to the brain, then cut through the nerves in the front section that control your personality and behaviour, and I read that it can have hellish side effects, like you could lose control of the bowel and bladder. So, now we'll have Lisa going along the high street with no control over those two organs, and screaming foul language at everyone she sees.'

'Steve, you're well read, but the trouble with the books you read is that they were written fifty years ago. The medical world has these treatments down to a fine art now. Lisa has her baby to think about. She can't go on wasting any more years and nor can I. I don't like to say it, Steve, but you have had your severe *SP* for so many years that it's the only life you know.'

'Maybe, Jack, but I still know there's a far better life out there, and OK my books are dated, but I have read about ECT and lobotomy, and to me it reads like a savage, brutal, horrific nightmare. OK, so for some unknown godforsaken reason we can't face people in certain situations, or most types of even minor social occasions. We live a life controlled by fear. It's a very depressing and debilitating illness, but to let some clown cut into my brain or send powerful electric shocks through my head causing me to go into a fit? No fucking way!'

At this, Bru started to bark loudly and Jack said, 'Calm down, Steve. Calm down. Have a whisky; it'll steady your nerves.'

'Why don't *you* have a double or treble instead of those electric shocks? Jack, you're my pal. I care about you, and Lisa's the daughter I never had.'

'Steve, you've had a life of hell and you're getting old. Just when do you think the good times are gonna start? When you see me on the mend, I bet you'll give ECT a try, too.'

Bru had stopped barking.

I knocked back the whisky, forced myself to calm down like Jack suggested, then gave him my reply.

'I don't think so, Jack, and I'll tell you why. As you rightly say, I'm getting old and I guess my views are dated, and man do I agree I've had *SP* for far too long, in fact most of my life, and I've had a shit of a life because of it. Now, there is one major fact you're not taking into account: none of the medical people who are treating us has ever suffered the hell of *SP*.'

'Steve, did the surgeon who fixed your ulcer have to have ulcers, too?'

'He knew how to fix it, I agree, but he didn't know the pain of having it. What I'm saying is that all that I have been through has made me an expert on the subject – not a medical expert, but still an expert. I regret with all my heart I don't as yet have a cure, but then neither do the doctors. There are expert doctors for every illness you can name, but the illnesses are still with us. They have not found a total cure for hardly any of them. Jack, our brains are OK; we are sitting in this pub having a drink; we're not a danger to anyone; we know exactly what we are doing and saying. But put us in certain social situations, and we go to pieces. If the fault lay in our brain, we would show those symptoms all the time, 24/7. Our hands, for example, would shake all the time, but right now they're perfectly steady. I know enough to know the answer doesn't lie in surgery or electricity; it lies within ourselves. Trust me, Jack. Me, you and Lisa will come through. Don't have any more electric shocks.'

'I'll give it some careful thought, captain. I promise.'

He then gave me a mock salute. 'Now, let's go into battle with a couple more beers.'

Later that night he drove me back to my place with complete confidence. He was a very good driver and had quick reactions, yet he thought his brain needed highly complex potently dangerous surgery.

Jack continued with the ECT, but, alas, his depression got rapidly worse.

I was pleased to hear that the hospital had turned Lisa down when she asked for a frontal lobe lobotomy. They told her it wasn't suitable for her type of illness, so she stopped going for treatment.

She brought Lara over to see me, and, would you believe, I actually went out and got a takeaway pizza. I was scared, but I did it. Lisa told me that evening that she needed a change of scene and was going to live with her sister in Eastbourne, a holiday town on the south coast.

As she left, she gave me a hug and said, 'If you get lonely, call and see Mum. She's always pleased to see you.'

The very next day I had to visit the hospital for an assessment of my own case. It was with a self-important looking young male doctor whom I had not seen before, with a bored nurse standing behind his chair. Peering over the rim of his glasses, he explained that they had to cut back on costs, and the therapy unit was being closed. I had responded fairly well to therapy, but not to long-term medication (I assumed by "long-term" he meant, all told, about twenty years!).

'So we must consider alternatives.'

'Like what?' I asked.

'Well, ECT. That's electric shock treatment.'

'Yes, I know what it is,' I replied.

'Or further down the line, even brain surgery.'

As he stood up, the nurse quickly took his jacket off the back of the chair and helped him on with it.

'I think you should try the ECT. Here, read through these and tell me next time what you have decided.'

He handed me some booklets about ECT, then he looked at his watch and, before the second hand had covered another thirty seconds, he was gone.

Outside, his secretary was sitting at her desk, gazing at a computer. I asked her to tell the great man that I'd given it some thought (about two minutes!) and ' ... call me a wimp, but ECT or surgery are not for me'.

Without looking up she said, 'I've made a note of that. 'Bye now.'

About a week later I received a letter saying my sickness benefit was being stopped at once because the hospital had informed them that I had refused treatment.

I kept reading and re-reading the letter. What on earth would I do now?

All that time, all those drugs, all that therapy had come to nothing, not only for me but for Jack and Lisa, and so many others.

I thought about Ben who could no longer work as a musician because he had damaged his hearing with loud noise, playing at rock concerts. This had caused severe tinnitus, a constant loud ringing sound inside his head that must surely be the ultimate in hell on earth. So, of course, he could no longer interact socially and had become deeply depressed.

And Julie, who had OCD (obsessive compulsive disorder). One day she would unbutton her coat, then button it up again, non-stop, all day long. The next day it would be something different, like combing her hair non-stop. This awful illness also destroyed her socially.

For these two, and many others, severe *SP* was an offshoot of their main illness, but, of course, like all of us, they could no longer take part in life. And like all of us they were hurting and suffering.

I looked forward to Lisa's letters in her copperplate handwriting. In one she had enclosed some photos that she'd taken in the park back in the summer. Looking at us sitting on the grass in the sun you would never dream such torment was going on inside our heads.

I called to see Jack when I felt well enough, but it wasn't the same. He was there, but his thoughts were miles away. I showed him Lisa's letter and photos, but for an awful moment he couldn't think who she was.

I'd noticed his old car parked in the street: it looked dirty and the tyres were going down. When I mentioned this he just said, 'I don't drive any more, Steve. That's why I've not been over to see you. In fact, I don't attend the hospital any more.'

'Tell you what, Jack,' I replied, 'I still have my driver's licence, so I'll drive. Let's go for a beer, and I'll put the car through the car wash and put some air in the tyres, and it'll give Bru a run at the same time.' At the sound of his name Bru, who was asleep on the floor, lifted his head.

'No, I don't feel up to it, pal. I feel all-in.'

I could see how tired he looked, so I told him I'd push off and would see him next week.

'No, don't go, Steve,' he said quickly. 'Stay and have a bite.'

I did, but he said very little the rest of the evening. Still, I'm pleased he was glad of my company.

Later, when I left, he said, 'You're a good pal. I'd have you in my platoon any day.' Then, using both his hands, he shook my right hand warmly.

The last bus had gone so I walked home that night, but had to run for my life to avoid a gang of violent yobs. I realised the London streets were now far too dangerous for night people like me. *SP* or not, I would have to start venturing out in daylight.

Only four days later I opened my door to a young police officer. I sensed by his grim look that it was bad news of some sort. He asked my name and some other details, then he quoted Jack's name, age and address.

'I understand you're a friend of the gentleman. Is that correct, sir?'

I nodded, dreading what he'd say next.

'I am very sorry to have to tell you, sir, that he has been found dead in his car.'

'Oh God no! Was it a car crash?' I asked.

'No, sir. He ran a hose from the exhaust into the car, closed all the windows, started up the engine and let it run.'

Apparently he had driven out into the Kent countryside, parked in a field and ended his life.

The policeman stayed for a while. I was so shocked that he even made me a cup of tea.

When he left I felt too dazed and stunned to cry. I just sat staring at the wall, thinking about my dear old pal

The funeral was over at the Verdant Lane crematorium in Catford. I dreaded going, but I wouldn't let Jack down. I stood right at the back of the church. The coffin was draped in the flag of St George and there were some soldiers there in uniform, looking very smart, representing his regiment. Jack would have liked that.

During the service I kept thinking that he had dodged bullets, shells, grenades, endured all sorts of hardships and survived, but he could not stand up to *SP*.

After the service I didn't speak to anyone and was about to walk quietly away when Mary appeared.

'Hello, Steve. I'm here to represent Lisa. She is devastated over this. She sends her love. Don't be alone today; come home with me for a meal.'

Less than a week later, I was in the flat writing a letter to my old firm asking if it still needed railway carriage cleaners – I was desperate as money for food was getting short – when someone knocked loudly on my door. The bell no longer worked because I couldn't afford to replace the batteries.

It was a woman I didn't know, with a dog I did. She was holding Bru on a lead attached to a very tight collar. Bru leapt up at me with excitement. I made a big fuss of him and invited the woman in.

144

Over tea she told me she was Jack's widow, Eve. She talked non-stop, and I got the impression that she wanted to move on with her new life and put closure on the past. She was living with a guy and wanted to marry soon. By the look of her clothes and jewellery, the new guy was wealthy.

I could see why Jack had been attracted to her – she must have been a real stunner – but her eyes were hard and she never once smiled. She would never understand or be able to help anyone with *SP*.

She answered my thoughts by saying, 'When I met Jack he was in the army. He fought in the Falklands war and other places. He jumped out of planes; nothing scared him. In hand-to-hand fighting he got bayoneted through the arm. He was a sergeant who stood on the parade ground giving out orders to his men. Then, one day, he's too scared to enter a restaurant, and, when it came to making a speech at our daughter's wedding, he shook so much he couldn't hold the paper he was trying to read from. That was the end of our marriage. Was he nuts, or what?'

After listening to her appraisal of *SP* I felt even more sorry for my old pal.

'No, he wasn't nuts, Eve,' I said. 'He had told me once, jokingly, "There is no such thing as sanity: only degrees of insanity." No, he was very sane. You see, like a person can have lung or heart trouble, with Jack and me our nerves have broken down. I can't give you a reason for it, but I'm working on it.'

She looked blank, then, changing the subject, said, 'would you have Bru? There's no place in my life for a dog, so he will have to be put down.'

Bru was looking at me with his head on one side, willing me to say 'Yes'.

'Sure. I'll give him a home.'

She got up to leave, saying, 'Great! Here, this will buy some dog food', and put what I thought was a £10 note in my hand. I was glad to see the back of her, but when I put on my reading glasses I realised it was a £50 note!

So, in the last half hour I had acquired a family and become financially solvent.

I loosened Bru's collar three notches and we went shopping. I bought soap, toilet rolls, washing powder, batteries, all the basic items I'd run out of. I even got a haircut.

Bru loved living with me. He would sit next to me on the settee while I read, or stand on his hind legs with his paws on the windowsill looking out at the passing traffic. At night he slept on the floor beside my bed, on his back with his legs in the air, sleeping the perfectly contented sleep. If only I could sleep like that, instead of dreaming a constant flow of anxious meaningless rubbish and waking every hour, like I'd done for years.

I would say to any *SP* sufferer: get a pet. It could be a dog, cat, parrot, rabbit or hamster. Open your heart to the animal kingdom. Animals can bring great joy, love and companionship into your lonely life. And it follows that if you have *SP*, you must be lonely.

Lately I had stayed away from the park. Going there alone I felt self-conscious, and other members of the public seemed to regard me with suspicion, but now, having Bru with me, I had a reason to be there. I was walking the dog; some fellow dog owners even wanted to stop and talk.

It was now more than three months since Jack had died and I had been spending about twenty-two out of every twenty-four hours indoors, surviving hand-to-mouth.

The slight improvement in my *SP* due to therapy was wearing off, so I was almost back to square one.

Another good reason to stay in was that I had nowhere to go and no one to see.

One good thing did happen: the health department found they had been paying me the wrong amount each week for about fifteen months, so they sent me £310 back pay. This was an absolute godsend.

I had no TV and never bought a newspaper; I had no interest in world events because I didn't regard myself as part of the normal everyday world.

My one pastime was reading. "Catman" was a keen reader and would return from the library laden down with books, and I would read most of them before he returned them.

Lisa had once given me a small transistor radio, so I did have a bit of music for company.

That, then, was my life. I stayed in my flat where I felt lonely, ill, poor, depressed ... but safe.

Lisa had not written for a while, so one evening I plucked up courage and took a bus ride over to see Mary.

There was no reply; the place seemed very quiet and there was no sign of her small van outside.

The next day I was to be dealt another blow that you never really recover from.

I came out of the park gates with Bru and saw Mary's van parked – it was hard to miss with her fashion shop logo on the side in bright colours.

'When you weren't at the flat I knew I'd find you here,' she said very quietly as I climbed in next to her.

'How are the two girls?' I asked, and it was then I saw the tears in her eyes.

'There's no easy way to tell you, Steve. Lara's fine, but her mum has gone. She's at peace now.'

For I don't know how long, I just sat there crying and moaning like some injured animal.

Mary took me to her place where I stayed in a dark haze of grief for a couple of days. She told me that Lisa had been getting slowly worse for the past few weeks and had tried to take Lara for her first day at school, but had shocked the other young mothers and the teachers who were present when she shouted out a string of obscenities at nobody in particular.

Within the hour she was on the train back to London, then went direct to Greenwich, climbed over the railings somewhere near the Cutty Sark and waded out fully clothed into the icy cold water, then slowly began to swim. Even strong swimmers can't last in the Thames. In no time she was in trouble, caught in the strong current.

Some guys on the landing stage saw what was happening and raced out to her in a fast motorboat, but they were too late; she was gone. The river police found her body later, a mile further downstream.

She left a note saying, 'No service, no flowers, and no mourners.'

I disobeyed her wishes and a week later I went down to where she got into the river and I threw a large bunch of flowers over the railings. They were soon swept away in the fast flowing river. Sometimes you must do the opposite of what the one who died wanted for your own sake. As Bru and I walked slowly back up the hill to the park, I thought what a very brave girl she was; I hope her and Jack are at peace now. I felt very proud to have had them both as friends and I'll miss them every day for the rest of my time.

I would spend ages each night in the phone box across the street, calling firms that took on night workers. Most times my age was against me, or they wanted to know what my last job was. When I said I had been unemployed for some time due to illness, they couldn't put the phone down fast enough.

Anyway, I knew that since the operation I wasn't fit enough for hard manual work any more, but with no money coming in I could hold out for only a few more days.

On my last night of phoning, I was walking back across the road with Bru when a scruffy-looking yob beggar stopped me and said, 'Give me the price of a drink, mate?'

I told him, 'I don't have any money myself, mate, for drink or anything else.'

He swore and moved towards me with his fist raised. Bru started to snarl and growl, then quickly moved between us with his ears flat to his head and showing a nasty set of large teeth. The yob would have attacked, but thought better of it and ran off into the night. I remember Jack saying Bru would defend you with his life.

Thinking about the incident back at the flat, over a cuppa, I had a brilliant idea or maybe a spell of madness,

I'm not sure which. For some reason, I recalled the beggars up at the railway station when I worked there as a cleaner. They would sit on the ground looking hopeless with their dogs, and people passing by on the way to the trains would drop a few pence into the hat they had beside them. Later, not looking anywhere near so hopeless, they would gather at the coffee stall, enjoying hot drinks and sandwiches.

The next day for breakfast I had some tea and toast – so that was the last of the bread – and Bru had some cat food that I had borrowed from "Catman" down the hall. We were now facing starvation, so that evening Bru and I set off to try our hand at begging in Charing Cross station. It's amazing what desperation can make you do.

Begging with Bru

Even in the depths of *SP*, I don't think I've ever felt so self-conscious as I did that night on entering the large busy booking hall of the station. I walked around for ages, too embarrassed and shaky to sit down and actually beg.

There were only two other rivals in the station that night: an old woman sitting on a mat by the taxi rank – she wore dark glasses and had a white stick, and a man who wandered around the concourse talking to people and constantly smiling – around his neck hung a card saying just one word: "Homeless", and on his shoulder sat a tiny pet monkey wearing a bright red jacket. When some kind-hearted soul stopped to give a few coins, the monkey would reach out and take them. This made people laugh, and kids would get their dads to give more money just to see the monkey do it again. *A bit too clever for you, Bru*, I thought to myself.

I finally decided: *it's now or never*, and sat down at the top of the flight of steps that led down to Villiers Street. Bru lay beside me with a look that said: *What the hell are we doing here?*

Nothing happened for some time, then a young guy dropped a fifty pence piece into my hand. I heard myself say, 'Thank you sir', like he had just paid for a £1,000 suit.

After about three hours I began to ache with the cold, and my takings were still under £20, but at least it would buy something to eat.

As I got up to leave, an Irish voice called out, 'How did you do then?' It was "Monkey Man". He held out his hand saying, 'I'm Dan Regan, and this is Mitzi.' He pointed to the monkey, now clinging to his arm.

'Hello. I'm Steve Conway,' I told him. Little did I realise that this meeting was going to prove momentous, and put me on the fast track for what I had been trying to do for nearly forty years ... free myself from the living hell of severe social phobia.

Like most Irish people, Dan was easy to talk to and could make you laugh. The conversation continued thus:

'Do you fancy a quick drink, Steve?'

'No thanks, Dan. I'm going to the stall to get a bite to eat for me and the dog.'

'Is that dog your friend?'

'Well, yes, he is.'

'Then what's his name?'

'He's called Bru.'

He bent down, took hold of Bru's paw and said, 'Hello, Bru. Nice to meet you.'

I was starting to think I'd run into yet another nutter, when he said, 'Y'know, Steve, we should take each day as a gift, like animals, birds and all natural things do. They can teach us a lot. You see, they are content just to be.'

As I approached the coffee stall, *SP* started to kick in; the usual stab of fear in the guts.

I turned to Dan, handed him the money, and said, 'would you get me a tea and a cheese roll, and a sausage roll for Bru? And please have a tea yourself.'

Without any questions he said, 'Sure I will.'

Bru and I tucked into our rolls, like we were starving.

Dan made no comment, but asked, 'How much did you make?'

'About eighteen quid,' I told him.

'Jesus, that's no good at all!' he yelled. 'You just got me a tea, so in exchange I'm going to give you a million pounds worth of advice. Now listen, my friend. You look ill, that's good. But you also look clean, that's no good. You have to let your hair grow long, and don't shave every day, and yer must have a notice.'

'A notice?' I repeated.

'Yes, indeed,' he said, pulling from inside his coat a selection of them with various slogans: "Please Help"; "Hungry & Cold"; "I've About Given Up". 'Ah, this is the one for you.' He thrust it into my hand. It read: "Too Ill To Work". 'Oh, and get rid of Bru's lead; it's too fancy. Get a bit of old rope.' Then he reached forward and grabbed the lapel of my jacket, and tore it so it hung down. 'That's better. The coat's old, but far too neat.'

With that, he went back to the stall and got two coffees. Handing me one he said, 'I'm a fraud, a likeable one, but a fraud, and I make fifty pounds a day. And my idea of a day's work is three to four hours. Now, you're genuine, so should make twice that.'

'Yes, Dan, but I don't have the gift of the gab like you do.'

He threw his head back, laughing, and said, 'The real name for it is "blarney".'

Then, looking into his cup at the last dregs of coffee, he threw them over my now torn jacket.

'When that dries, you'll have a lovely dark stain. See? You're starting to look the part already. I'll see yer tomorrow, m'boy. Now don't forget: bring a cushion to sit on, and a dish so Bru can have a drink of water.'

With that, he darted off into the crowds of people heading for their trains, with Mitzi still on his shoulder gazing back at Bru who returned her puzzled look. I guess beggar's assistants have a mutual understanding of one another.

When I arrived at the station the next day, I was disappointed not to see Dan and, of course, Mitzi doing their usual routine. So I sat with my head down in the same place, on the small cushion that on Dan's good advice I'd brought with me, and with a dish of water by my side for when Bru got thirsty. I sat head down because I hated making eye contact with the people going past.

The truth of the matter was that I felt ashamed of what I was doing, even though the notice around my neck – "Too Ill to Work" – was the truth.

Many going past would drop a coin or two into my cap, then ask what my illness was; perhaps they thought it might be catching. This, of course, made me blush, stutter and get confused, as I tried to tell them about my stomach operation, which did, indeed, make me feel ill and very weak at times. They meant well, so I spared them the ordeal of hearing me try to explain SP, the illness that was really incapacitating me.

Not often, but some days, I could sit there for more than three hours and go home empty-handed, yet on another; more lucky, day the same amount of time could bring in around £30.

The very best day ever was down to a smart looking American in a lightweight suit. He stood looking at me for a while, then said, 'How much for the hound?'

'Sorry, sir,' I said. 'He's not for sale.'

The man smiled, and came back with, 'What say, ten thousand dollars?'

I put my hand on Bru's head, and said, 'Not even for a million. You see, sir, I have nothing in my life, if I did have I wouldn't be sitting here, but I do have him, my best friend, and might I ask what you would want him for? Maybe your ranch back home?'

He laughed again, more loudly. 'That bag of bones would be more trouble than he's worth where I come from. No, I just like testing people.'

He shook my hand, and then said, 'Here. You passed the test.'

With that he put five $100 bills in my hand.

I called out, 'God bless you', as he walked away still laughing. (I never have worked out what, exactly, his test was all about.) I couldn't believe my luck because, at that time, those dollars were worth around £270.

I put my cushion and Bru's dish in my carrier bag, and went straight over to a *bureau de change* in the Strand to change the dollars into pounds. My hand trembled as I gave the cash over the counter, and I felt the usual *SP* confusion and panic sweep over me, but I forced myself to pick up the pound notes no matter how much I shook.

Later that same week, Dan was back strolling around with Mitzi on his shoulder, talking to people waiting for their trains, who were seeing loved ones off or waiting to greet them.

I watched in admiration the way he approached everyone with such an easy charm. It could be a rough crowd of football fans or the most stately looking old lady who probably had a Rolls waiting in the car park.

He had this gift of starting a conversation with anyone, as though he had known them all his life. Sometimes his greeting would be met with abuse (putting it very politely, he would be told to 'clear off'), but nothing seemed to faze him.

He was a tall impressive looking man in his mid-forties with a friendly face, but you also sensed this was not a man to try and push around, and I never saw anyone silly enough to threaten him. As I found out, beggars do get threats and abuse from the public. A few times yobs would kick my legs and swear at me as they passed; it would have happened more often, but I had Bru with me, and I now know that the reason most street beggars have a dog for company is for protection.

One night, the police had a purge on beggars. They decided there were too many of them, and ordered us to move on. The others meekly packed up their pathetic little bundles and started to move off. Not Dan. He approached the police officer in charge and explained (if that's the right word) that he and his 'friend Steve over there', pointing at me, were not beggars at all but street entertainers. He went on to explain that there was a whole world of difference between the two: in fact, we were more closely connected to the acting profession and the world of showbiz, and he had just finished appearing at some top entertainment centres in London!

I couldn't believe three or four high-ranking police officers were listening intently to this nonsense. His speech ended with laughs all round and the officers shaking hands with him. He came over to me, beaming, and said, 'I've made a deal. We push off now, but can come back discreetly in a couple of days and nothing will be said. Now, Steve, m'boy, let's go up Soho and have a drink.'

For the first time in God knows how long, I was doubled up with laughter.

Yet another surprise awaited me in the car park. He flicked the remote control key as we came up to an expensive looking, four wheel drive people-carrier.

'Don't tell me this is yours, Dan,' I said.

'T'be sure, it is! You need a tough motor if you're going back and forth to Ireland, like I do.'

After 40 Years It's Over

He drove us to a nice quiet pub near Soho Square. Everyone on both sides of the bar knew Dan, and, by the way the pretty barmaid fluttered her eyelashes at him, he was very popular. When she came over to our table with a whisky for me, Guinness for Dan and a round of sandwiches, I said, 'This is on me, my friend' as I paid her.

'Thank you. I'm honoured.'

I must have looked puzzled because he went on, 'Honoured that you regard me as a friend. We all need friends in this world, and how.'

I had already told him about my lucky break with the American who wanted to buy Bru.

'So,' he told the barmaid, 'my good friend, Steve here, turned down an offer of a million dollars for his dog.'

She looked down at Bru and said, 'I would have taken an offer of ten quid.'

'The trouble with you, m'girl, is you're not on the same wavelength as the animal kingdom. I would never part with Mitzi for a million, either.'

Mitzi seemed pleased to hear this; she was in a small bag where Dan kept her inside his coat, with just her head looking out.

The barmaid must have been slightly on Mitzi's wavelength because she came over with a bag of crisps for her.

It was great to sit here drinking with Dan. The whole atmosphere was relaxing; I felt at ease in his company, and so far, no sign of *SP* rearing its ugly head.

'Dan, why do you travel back to Ireland? I thought you lived here?'

'Ah, no,' he laughed, 'I live in north London with my daughter and her family when I'm over here, but this is my real home.' He took a photo out of his wallet and handed it to me: it showed a modern bungalow with a garden full of lovely flora.

It looked as though it might be abroad, so jokingly I said, 'don't tell me, Dan. This is your place in the south of France, right?'

'No, it's in Kinsale in county Cork, Ireland. Have you ever been there, Steve?'

'No, Dan, I never have. In fact, for nearly forty years I've not been out of the London area. Tell me, where were the top entertainment places you told those police you had been appearing in?'

'Oh, all over town. Last week I was appearing in Euston, Waterloo, Kings Cross.'

'Dan, they're main line railway stations. You made them sound like theatres.'

'Did I?' he said, with a smile. 'Well, I can't help the way people interpret what I say.'

'Mind you, I think you're wasted in stations. You should be at the London Palladium. But why do it, Dan?'

'Well, I like it. I can make good tax-free money for what, a twenty-hour week, and it's not what you'd call back-breaking work. I've got two married sons back in county Cork; my wife has all her family around her. Surely it's got to be better than working at some jobs we can think of?'

I thought about my public toilet cleaning, and agreed.

'I'm a free spirit, Steve. I like to be able to roam, not only physically but in my thoughts as well. My family back home are quite well known. Have you heard of Hanora Regan?'

'No, I can't say that I have. Is she a relative?'

'She's my sister: a famous clairvoyant and mystic. She helps people from all over the world. It all goes back a long way. Our grandmother travelled the south and southwest of Ireland in the 1930s in a donkey and cart, telling fortunes and reading palms at the fairs.'

'I'm surprised you don't try that at the station, Dan.'

'Oh, I could do. Like all my family, I'm gifted with what we call second sight, but better not push our luck with the police. Mind you, if they do get heavy we'll move on to Victoria station. That's a damn good pitch. They arrive there from Brighton: plenty of money down there. Hey, have another one. What'll you have?'

When he returned with the drinks, I said, 'Better not include me in any long-term plans, Dan. I'm only doing this because I was broke. As soon as I find something ... '

'You'll do what? He asked.

I couldn't think of a quick answer.

'Steve, be honest with yourself. Never lie to yourself; it's a form of suicide.'

'Sadly, I've tried that, too,' I told him.

'That doesn't surprise me at all. You see, Steve, you're not going anywhere. You have tried everything, and there is nowhere left to go now, is there? Be honest.'

'How do you know so much about me?'

'I told you. I have second sight. I may not know the small details, but I see the general picture. You need to talk to someone, right? So talk to me, then I'll tell you what to do about your problems.'

I suddenly felt embarrassed, and tried to joke my way out.

'Will I have to cross your palm with silver for all this, Dan?'

'Yes. I'm after some of those dollars you got the other day,' he laughed, and raised his glass. 'It will only cost you the price of another packet of crisps for Mitzi.'

Don't ask me why, but for some reason – maybe the drinks I'd had ... but no, there I go making silly jokes again. I was perfectly sober. I told him my life story, all in under fifteen minutes.

I explained how in my early twenties I had a flat near this pub and a great job. Then I explained the strange symptoms and utter horrors of *SP* and losing Kate - all the different treatments I'd tried, and the drugs I'd been given over the long years; how dear friends, like Lisa and Jack, had met tragic deaths as a result of the same illness; my suicide attempt and, as a result, the breakdown in my general health; the hell of trying to recover from major ulcer surgery; the long years spent hiding from the daytime world in my miserable flat, only able to come out at night to clean toilets or railway carriages; to be denied all the things that others take for granted: a decent home and family, and, by now, grandchildren ... it must be the ultimate in life-destroying, long-term lonely illness.

'In fact, I haven't had a life. I have only existed.'

Dan looked thoughtful, then said; 'Right, my friend, go and get Mitzi those crisps you promised her. Don't ask me to get them: one, because it's your round; and two, because there is no valid reason on earth why you can't go up to the bar, and get two more drinks and a packet of crisps, now is there?'

I got up and went over to the bar. When I got there, Dan's barmaid friend said, 'same again?'

I nodded ... so that part was easy. When I paid, she did not appear to notice my trembling hands. Then I had to get the drinks back to our table. Somehow I managed it, and sat down with a sigh. I handed Mitzi a large crisp and gave a handful to Bru. Mitzi fixed me with her bright tiny eyes, and took the crisp very gently, instead of her usual snatch.

Dan sat staring into his drink, then said, 'Of course, I knew seventy-five per cent of your story already. I spotted it the first day we met, when you gave me the money to get the teas at the station. My theory is that you have a very low opinion of yourself, but I'm going to double-check. Let's get some expert women's intuition on the subject; it's the same as theory, but with them it's intuition.'

He took out a mobile phone and tapped in a number. Then, leaning back with a broad smile, he said, 'Hello, m'darling, how are yer? Yes, she's fine. Sure, isn't she next to me right now, having some crisps?'

I carried on with my drink, and looked around at the others in the bar chatting and laughing, and I thought how seldom I had done anything like this over the years. I overheard bits of Dan's conversation like: 'my friend, Steve here, has a problem. He's a man who has suffered a lot. The doctors have done nothing for him, except line their pockets. Sure, he's English, but he can't help that, now can he?'

With that, he roared with laughter at his own joke, making those at the bar look over at us. The barmaid winked and smiled, as much as to say, 'Is Dan up to his tricks again?'

After about twenty minutes, he put the phone back in his pocket and said, 'Good news. After a lifetime of hell, you will suffer no more or I'll want to know the reason why. That was my sister – Hanora, in Ireland – that I told you about. She has cured dozens like you. She's an expert on panic attacks, shyness, blushing, stammering, depression, you name it. She should be available on the British NHS (*National Health Service*). She would put some of those fancy white coat merchants, who forget your name as soon as you leave their consulting rooms, out on their arses. Ask yourself why they forget your name: because they have no real interest in you, or your case. You are the only one with a real interest. Think about it.

'This is what you must do, Steve. It won't be easy because it means changing the way you have regarded yourself for almost a lifetime. You have to change the way you think. It's like you have been brainwashed by yourself and accepted without question what you told yourself. Now you must undo all that. Think of a nation that has been brainwashed by a political doctrine or type of government, then one day the dictator gets assassinated and it all changes overnight. Then it's: "No, we don't do it like that any more. Now, we do it like this." You know deep in your heart, as well as I do, these things that terrify you are not dangerous or frightening at all and there is nothing to be scared of. Right?'

'I agree, Dan, but what you or your sister is suggesting is easier said than done.'

'Bullshit! Once it is done, your life will be a hell of a lot easier. You have spent years subconsciously hoping other people, like psychiatrists, would help you. Well, this way you do it yourself, by yourself and for yourself. You become your own best friend. For years, you have been your own worst enemy, your own cruel critic. You have been your own judge and jury, and you always find yourself guilty, then sentence yourself to death, a living death with severe social phobia. Deep in your mind, Steve, you regard other people as better than you. For a very long time now, you have hated being you. OK, so you're no better than anyone else, but then, by the same token, no one is better than you. When you're faced with some self-important idiot, just remember the graveyards are packed with absolutely indispensable, very important people.

'You have to re-think your outlook. Not easy, but it can – *and must* – be done. You must learn to love yourself. I don't mean going around thinking, "I'm the greatest". That's silly vanity. No, I mean love yourself because you are all you have and ever will have, so be happy with that. Break the habit of a lifetime. From now on, you never put yourself down. You can be very proud of the way you've stood up to your illness all these years, when others, like your friends, have sadly fallen by the wayside.'

Just then, Dan's phone rang. He greeted the caller, then, handing the phone to me, said, 'Hanora wants a word.'

'Hi, Steve. Sure, I want you to tell me something, if you will.'

Her voice had the same friendly quality that her brother's had, like she had known you for years.

'Yes, ask me anything you like.'

'Well, what do you think you would be doing now if your phobia had not struck you down when you were a young man?'

I had to think carefully for a moment, then gave my answer.

'The owner of the flat I rented here in Soho offered it to me for four thousand pounds, a lot of money back then, but I could have got a loan and paid it off in a couple of years. Today, it would set you back around a million. The man I worked for was talking about making me a partner. He died many years ago and had no family. So today, I would probably own one of the most exclusive tailor shops in Mayfair, and would be very wealthy. I would, of course, have married and had a family. In short, I would have had a very good life.'

'Yes, just what I thought,' said Hanora slowly. 'Your way of thinking is all-wrong. You're sending incorrect and misleading messages to your brain that make you feel and act the way you do. Have you thought that as a young man, when you crossed Regent Street one day on the way to work, you could have been knocked down by a bus? Then you and I would not be having this chat, and you wouldn't

173

be enjoying a drink with Dan in that pub. You can't live a dream life, Steve. I agree life dealt you a rough hand, but now you have an ace up your sleeve. You now have the means of turning things around.

'Another thing: be upfront about your phobia. If I had one – about going up in a plane, or spiders – I'd tell everyone. I wouldn't try to hide it. Trying to hide something that big in your life is impossible, causes great stress and makes the whole thing ten times worse, if that's possible.

'You must think of yourself now as a man who has just been released from prison after serving forty years for a crime he did not commit. You'll be surprised at the number of people who will help you, if you explain to them about your problem. The world's moved on since you went into hiding so many years ago; people are more enlightened now. And if you run into those who won't help or can't understand ... who needs them? Not you.

'Remember, God made you, and you did – and are doing – the best job you can with the tools you've got.

'You'll have setbacks, but when they happen, say, "OK, so I trembled, blushed, stuttered, got totally embarrassed"; you name it, you did it. So what? It's not the end of the world. You will still be here the next day, and the day after that. Those people who were present, when you got into a state, have their own private horrendous problems that they are far more concerned about than they are about you.

'Once you start thinking this way, Steve, you can only get better. You will soon be in the real world again, one you have been out of for far too long. You will, most likely, stay a reserved sort of person, and social events will not be your favourite pastime, but they will not be the fearful nightmare to you that they are right now. You won't go overnight from lonely recluse to all-round entertainer.

'Remember; love yourself in a quiet, calm way. Be proud of even the smallest successes you have. Never put yourself down; write off your failures. Be happy with yourself and, above all, be happy being you. It won't be easy, but, starting today, you can – *and must* – do it. Then it will be the end of your fear, anxiety, dread, and misery ... the end of your social phobia.'

I thanked Hanora and tried to tell her how much her help meant to me. Then I handed the phone back to Dan with a very shaky hand, not because of *SP* but with emotion. I sat stunned, realising that she and Dan had got it absolutely right.

'You look shocked, my friend, said Dan. 'I'll get you a drink.'

'No, Dan. I'll get them.'

As I handed Dan his Guinness, I told him that he and his sister were truly remarkable.

'Not really, Steve. You see, we're peasants who are in touch with the spiritual world.'

'Peasants don't own lovely bungalows and drive people-carriers,' I kidded him.

Looking around him, he replied, 'Take the good folk in this bar. I know most of them. They're a great crowd, but they have never been really hungry. They wear nice clothes, live in warm houses, and get their food from the supermarket. They have never dug their potatoes out of the ground, never chopped wood for a fire, never delivered a baby or laid out the dead. Well, my grandmother and mother did all those things. We lived off our little bit of land facing the harsh Atlantic; we grew most of our own food, and kept ducks, chickens and geese. We were in touch with the elements − earth, wind, rain and fire − and, therefore, in touch with ourselves. That's what today's people have lost, and it's what happened to you, Steve: you lost touch with yourself.'

I went back to the bar, and borrowed a pen and some sheets of paper. While it was still fresh in my mind, I wrote down almost word for word all that Hanora and Dan had told me.

From that day forth I tried with all my heart and mind to think in this new way. It wasn't easy, and, as Hanora had warned, there were setbacks, but gradually this way of thinking became the new me.

Well, within three months, I was 95 per cent cured. All the things and situations that were impossible for me a few weeks before, I could now do.

I kept in touch with Dan, but I stopped begging at the station.

Mary asked me to help her on her clothing stall at the covered market. I drive to the wholesaler in the van to pick up the stock; I serve customers at the stall, chat with them, take the money, give the change; talk business with the other stallholders. I am out there living a life.

I gave up my flat and let dear old "Catman" have all the furniture because Mary and I decided to live together. It's an autumn love, but a real nice one. We are bringing Lara up together. She's now a lively teenager who shows no sign of her mother's illness. Whenever she asks about Lisa, I tell her how brave she was and to be so proud of her memory.

I still take Bru to the park – not so often now because he's very old and I have to lift him into the car. Taking him on when Jack died was one of the best things I ever did. He shared a lot of those hard, bleak years with me, and means more to me than I can put into words.

I even take Mary out for a night up town every couple of weeks. We get a cab to the West End to see a show, and later have a meal in a restaurant or maybe a drink in a bar. Sometimes, we go with friends from the market.

I don't shake or blush or show any of the old signs of *SP*. If you saw me, you'd take me to be a calm, at ease, laid back type of person, and you'd be right: I am.

Dan keeps asking us to go over to Ireland for a holiday and meet Hanora. So, just yesterday, I booked the flight. I'm looking forward to it, no problem.

I saw a reader's letter in the paper about *SP* from a sufferer, so I replied, giving some advice. From that, I was asked by the people who run a phobic society if I would come along and give a talk. Can you imagine that!

Well, I went, and there were about forty sufferers present. As I stood up to say my few words, the old fear and terror hit me, but in a much more diluted form, and it quickly subsided. I started by saying, 'Can you bear with me for an hour or so until I stop shaking?' That broke the ice, and I said my bit; it lasted about twenty minutes. Would you believe, I even cracked a couple of jokes? As I sat down, to my amazement – and I admit, delight – I got a round of applause. OK, not a standing ovation, but who knows, maybe next time? I wish you could have been there. They even asked me to come back, and I now give talks to *SP* sufferers on a regular basis.

So, no matter what type of social occasion or mixing with other people you throw at me, I can handle it. I may not do it all that well, but the major point I am making is that I can now do it because of the way I think now.

And if I can do it, then surely anyone can, and that definitely includes *you*.

As an ex-sufferer, I urge you to suffer social phobia no more and to get well.

To be contented and free from excessive worry, and at peace in your own mind, is your birthright.

I wish you well, my friend.

Remembering Kate

When the first smaller edition of this book was published in 2005 I received hundreds of letters from readers worldwide to say how the book had helped them deal with their own *SP*.

For years I thought mine must be the worst case of the illness, in its severest form, but I have learnt that many have suffered even more than I have, and many cases were truly horrendous. I tried to answer every letter that the publisher forwarded to me because being able to help even in a small way means everything to me.

However, one letter from America helped me to find some peace of mind and put a ghost to rest that had haunted me for almost as long as *SP*, and had caused me almost as much mental pain (although of a very different sort).

It was from a guy called Tim Halland who lives in Phoenix, Arizona. He had what he called mild *SP* but lived in fear of it getting much worse; but not anymore, my book had enabled him to get it under control. He went on to say that he often travelled on business to the adjoining state of New Mexico and the city of Santa Fe. This was, of course, the state that Kate had sent her last post card from and where I assume she lived. He kindly went on to say that if I sent all the details I could recall about her (for example; her age, full name etc) he would try and find out what had happened to her so long ago.

His letter had a phone number so I called him at once and he answered. I gave him all the info I could about Kate. He sounded young and had a friendly voice, so when he said he would do all he could I believed him. I then sat back in my chair dazed.

Could I at last be close to knowing what happened to the love of my life?

As I've related earlier in this book, when *SP* had crushed me and brought me to a suicidal state I had tried to take my own life. As I drifted in and out of consciousness I somehow knew Kate had already gone before me and was close by, waiting.

A month and five days later a padded airmail envelope arrived from the USA. Tim had written a five-page letter telling me all I longed to know. Tears blinded me as I read that Kate had collapsed and died in her cousin's car in the hospital car park. She had been to visit her mother who had passed away while Kate was there. It was a terrible shock for her of course, but it was revealed later that she had been born with a heart defect like her mother.

Tim had also located her cousin Leanne, now elderly and living in L.A. He enclosed some photos of the family grave where Kate, her mother and father all lay. I could read clearly the names and dates, but the grave looked overgrown and uncared for. So I phoned Tim to thank him and asked if he could arrange for someone to tidy up the grave and clean the marble stone. I also asked if he would put some roses (Kate's favourite flowers) there and I sent him a card to put with them in my hand writing saying;

"Kate. Love Always Steve."

He did all this and even several weeks later sent a new photo taken on a sunny day of the grave looking tidy and bright with my flowers against the stone. When I look at that photo I feel close to her again.

Tim was reluctant to accept any payment but I insisted on sending a cheque to cover all his expenses. If I had sent him a million pounds it would have been worth it to me. It just goes to show that there are still a few decent people left in this awful world.

When I phoned Leanne her accent reminded me of Kate's. She told me how Kate had shown everyone my photo and told them about her English boyfriend who was soon to be her husband. When she died they had no way of contacting me, all they had was 'Steve who lives in London' and they could find no trace of her London address.

Leanne cried as she said how good it was to be able to talk to me and explain what had happened on that terrible day so long ago; 'she got in my car right next to me, gave a long sigh then slumped forward and the poor girl was gone. I guess you're married and have a family Steve?'

'No, I have no one,' I said. Then, trying to avoid the topic of *SP* I added; 'I've had very poor health most of my life.'

We talked some more, then I thanked her so much for telling me what had happened.

If it had not been for a crippling attack of *SP* preventing me from going to the party that night at Kate's firm, I would have been with her when she got the news about her mother being ill. Then we would have flown out to the

States together. Who knows if me being with her would have prevented the heart attack?

SP can destroy one's life in so many strange and far-reaching ways. I like to think that she would be proud and pleased to know I'd finally overcome such a destructive, crippling condition.

Social Phobia in Hollywood

World famous Hollywood movie stars are not the first people you think of when thinking about those who suffer with severe social phobia.

Well, think again because Daryl Hannah star of "Blade Runner" and "Kill Bill" (who to date has made over seventy movies) was a chronic sufferer. She has told many times how she hated being young and did not really free herself of *SP* until she was around thirty.

As a young person she suffered from crippling shyness and would visibly shake if she had to speak to a stranger. Her teachers thought she needed psychiatric treatment (I could have told them to avoid that at all costs). Even today she does not feel at ease appearing live on stage, and fainted with fear when she had to appear on a live TV chat show; 'I lived my life in a vacuum of fear and dread of the next social occasion,' she said.

Daryl found an escape in acting. In this way she says she could lose her unhappy self by becoming another person. She came from a wealthy, protected background so one would expect her to have been a confident young person, but no, I have found that *SP* can strike anyone, at any time.

Daryl got well by immersing herself in the craft of acting, and for her this worked. She says rather sadly; 'I would not want my early years back at any price.'

She also has a great love of animals and finds their companionship very therapeutic (as I have done with dear old Bru).

Daryl is living proof that *SP* can be overcome and one can go on to be very successful. We must all be grateful to her for going public about suffering the hell of *SP*.

Her way out was acting, your own way will be something else. You see, unlike most other illnesses, the *SP* sufferer will tell themselves that there is no way out, no cure. This train of thought drags you down even further and it's wrong. Watch one of Daryl's movies and say to yourself; 'she had *SP*, just like me, and now look at her. So I can get well.'

Very similar to Daryl's theory of becoming another person when playing a part is the case of another great movie actor who made some classic movies in the 1940's through to the1970's; the late Raymond Massey. He was severely wounded and suffered shell shock during the First World War. This left him with a very pronounced stutter for the rest of his life. Because of this he became shy and withdrawn, a form of *SP*, yet on stage and in front of the camera he spoke in a calm, clear and firm voice with no trace of a stutter.

Raymond played strong characters on screen with no trace of shyness. When asked why this was, he said; 'because I'm not me anymore, I lose myself in the person I'm playing.'

This sounds very similar to Daryl Hannah's; 'I leave my unhappy self behind.' This really boils down to wanting to be another person. Anyone will do as long as it's not you. Why? Simply because you don't like or even hate yourself. This is where my cure comes in as Dan's sister Hanora told me you *must start to love yourself.*

OK, start by liking yourself then move on to love. Stop beating yourself up, forgive yourself for whatever you may have done in the past, and move on and like I've told you before, *become your own best friend.* Whether they realised it or not, that is exactly what movie stars Daryl

Hannah and Raymond Massey did. It is also what you must do to get well. Start today and let *SP* become part of your past.

Let's face it, life's hard enough without the self-inflicted hell of *SP* (and it is indeed, to a large extent, self inflicted).

One case of severe *SP* spinning out of control with disastrous and long lasting results was movie star Gene Tierney. Due to *SP* her life became a Hell on Earth. Darryl F. Zanuck, the founder of 20th Century Fox, said she was *'unquestionably the most beautiful woman in movie history'*, and few would argue with that.

Of Irish descent, she came from a wealthy East Coast family and was educated at private schools in Switzerland. Her looks got her stage work on Broadway at the tender age of 18. At 20 a Hollywood screen test proved she had what the studio called *a very intelligent screen presence and superb acting ability*. She was now on her way to becoming a screen legend.

It's well worth trying to catch one of her movies that are often shown on late night TV. She made over thirty, plus others made for TV, to name a few superb examples; "Whirlpool", "Leave Her to Heaven" and the all time cult classic "Laura". Gene co-starred with most of the leading male stars of Hollywood's golden era, and had affairs with two of the richest men on earth; Howard Hughes and Prince Aly Khan. She almost made it to the White House when she and Senator (later to become President) John F. Kennedy became an item. Wealthy, famous, beautiful, with fabulous homes in L.A and N.Y, well that's about as good as it gets! Or was it?

At the age of 37, in 1958, we find her standing on the narrow window ledge of her luxury New York apartment, about to end her misery by jumping down to east 57th street, 14 floors below. One of the N.Y cops who were called to the scene said; *one strong gust of wind up there would have been her death sentence*'.

Married to a successful fashion designer, their first daughter was born mentally retarded. A terrible blow to both Gene and her husband, and some say the reason for her future illness. However, I don't buy that, she was showing signs of *SP* long before her daughter was born. To find the real reason for her death wish, we must back track about 15 years when she realised she could no longer face an audience as herself.

As an actress playing a part with a script and fellow actors, Gene felt safe, even secure. But when appearing as herself she froze solid and couldn't speak. After previously acting as hostess at glittering social occasions and Hollywood parties, she now found it a hellish ordeal just to enter a room with a few people. She stated that *'most of the time I have a feeling of fear and I don't know why'.*

Most *SP* sufferers wonder at times if they are losing their minds, and because of that train of thought they feel very vulnerable and Gene was no exception. So, foolishly, she put herself in the hands of Psychiatrists, who no doubt smelt money (and if they played their cards right it could be long-term, big money). They convinced her she needed hospital treatment. Her family were mystified by her strange illness and didn't know what to do for the best. They stupidly signed the papers to have poor Gene committed to a psychiatric hospital.

Treatment for such illness in the 1940's and 50's was cruel and barbaric, so worse was to come because Gene was now a prisoner, locked in a cell 24/7, ill-treated and abused by the staff. It's a mistake, she said, to think people are drawn to the medical profession because they are kind and compassionate by nature. Quickly forgotten by her rich and powerful friends, frightened and confused, she agreed to have E.C.T treatment. In her own words: *'Today to my eternal regret I received my first electric shock treatment'*.

Over the next five years she would have that shock treatment no less than thirty-two times; as a result whole chunks of her life would be erased from her memory. Most of those years she would be confined within three different hospitals. Every cent of her huge earnings from movies would be eaten up by the horrendous cost of private medical treatment that lasted, all told, over 8 years.

When at last she made a screen comeback her acting was slightly wooden, and her face, through still lovely, was more set, less mobile and had lost some sensitivity. There was also an underlying sadness to her expression, all due of course to the massive amount of E.C.T treatment she had endured.

Gene gave up her career, married again, and retired to Texas. On medication for the rest of her life, she found a happiness of sorts, but never totally overcame *SP*. She was, in her time, adored by an International audience; women envied and copied her, powerful and famous men were in love with, her but *SP* still indirectly destroyed her. OK, I'm talking with 20/20 vision hindsight, but also as a sufferer of 40 years, and I say Gene's tragedy was that she did not love herself. If only she had, her life would have been totally different, and that applies to all *SP* sufferers.

Quotations, Sayings and Proverbs.

Over the long years I spent reading books in my lonely room I recall a few quotes at random that can sum up my story better than any footnote could do. Whether you my friend are a phobic sufferer or not it may give you pause for thought, I hope so.

Advice for all victims of phobias.

"Take each day as a gift, like animals birds and all natural things do. They can teach us a lot their content just to be. Do what you can and trust that someone or something will see to the rest because we never know what is waiting to morrow."

"Do the best job you can with the tools you have, that's all you can do,"

"That dreadful time of waiting and nervous suspense is the worst torment of all mental stress it breaks more hearts than sorrow. Causes more defeats than armed force one has to be strong to stand it."

"I feel so sorry for those who suffer phobias it's such a long term illness. They drag themselves along; it kills all enjoyment in life. Nothing seems to mean very much to them anymore,"

"Survivors understand one another."

"The depressed will grasp onto anything they can, and hold on to it for dear life."

"No power so effectually robs the mind of all its power of acting and reasoning as fear."

"You who are crying now what did you do with your youth."

Lisa telling me about her illness, Tourette's syndrome.

"I won't even try and explain to you how terrible it is to suffer this illness. However good your imagination and however hard I tried I know I'd fail."

To all the medical people I have met over the long years.

"The alleviation of suffering is paramount and everything should be devoted to such work."

Medical snobbery, the amount of money you are making, and your own self-importance. MUST be put aside for the sake of the patient

When I think of Lisa, Jack and all the other sufferers who never made it.

"All things once are things forever. Therefore a soul once living lives forever."

"When people are down and beaten, you see such kindness and respect for each other".

When I think about that brief love affair with Kate.

"There are moments in my life and places in my heart that I cannot forget."

"Love is measured not in moments of time, but in timeless moments."

"There is a place in our hearts and a time in our lives that will always be remembered."

"Forever young you'll always be deep within my memory, and though the sands of time may race, for me they'll never change your face. And though I'll grow old and grey. Forever young you will stay."

"Giving up lost hopes and dreams is very hard, but it's what you have to do. You must try and move on with you life or face an awful downward spiral of depression anger and sadness."

When I think of my life today.

"The supreme happiness of life is the knowledge that we are loved."

When I think about Bru.

"Dogs are not our whole life but they make our lives whole."

"A dog is like an eternal Peter Pan, a child who never grows old and who therefore is always available to love and be loved."

"There is something to be said at how quickly a dog makes friends in comparison to a human".

And when I think about you, my reader friend.

"There is a great escape to be found deep inside the pages of a book to anywhere you want to go. And the road to knowledge begins with the turn of a page."

And finally a small tribute to Billy Curtis I met him at the clinic, a charming interesting man to talk to he had travelled the world and was very well read. His S.P was so bad that he never left the house except when his wife brought him to the clinic by car. He had great hopes when he started therapy and wrote a little poem on a scrap of paper that I kept. It deserves to be published because I heard many years later that Billy took an overdose in 2001. Sadly his S.P had become so bad that he could not visit his wife in hospital or attend her funeral. And without her could not go on.

"I'll face the world though my hearts in pain, I'll put a smile upon my face, and deal with what's thrown at me to day, and each day as it passes my strengths will start to break through, and I'll no longer be a phobic, I'll be as strong as you. God bless and help all phobics in their fight."

Medical Notes

If you asked two people to tell you in detail about a serious illness – one the person who suffered it (the patient) and the other a doctor (or some other type of qualified medical person) – you would get two totally different descriptions of that illness.

The medical person would, of course, claim to have a far greater knowledge of the subject.

Technically speaking that's true of course, but the sufferer has, in my opinion, a greater knowledge coming from a very different source. An emotional knowledge: a feeling of fear; misery; extreme depression. Above all, he or she feels the pain, be it physical or mental, and knows only too well the dreadful effect that it has on his or her life.

The illness we are discussing here, of course, is "severe social phobia" (*SP*).

As a sufferer I've had forty years' experience of it... longer than most doctors have been in medicine.

I have made it clear from the beginning that I am not medically qualified in any way, so the following is a very general outline of some of the medical treatments available.

For more detailed advice, you should speak with your doctor.

To be honest, I was always scared and suspicious of these treatments – maybe because of the awful side-effects many of my friends and fellow sufferers experienced – and all the different drugs I was given over the years never helped me.

One must take into account that over so many years treatments for *SP* might have improved, and new types of treatment are, hopefully, coming onto the market every day. It would be great to know that one day, if a young person is struck down with *SP*, the medical people could clear it up with a simple course of tablets, instead of that person being disabled for life in the way that I and so many others were.

As you now know, in the end I found a cure (better late than never) that worked for me. If it works for you, or at least helps you, then I'm more than pleased.

Your salvation from *SP*, however, may come to you from some other direction or medical treatment.

What you must never do is give up. You must always strive for your personal cure. It's out there waiting for you, I promise. If I found it, then so can you, so can anybody.

The following are just some general descriptions and information on the illnesses that have been mentioned in this book. But, as I've said before, for much more detailed information about your individual case, you must seek medical advice.

Let's start with an official description of what this book is all about. The dictionary describes it like this: *A phobia is a persistent, excessive, irrational fear of an object, place or situation.*

My comment on that is, 'Man, you can say that again, because ain't that the truth.'

When I first went for hospital treatment for my strange and frightening condition all those years ago, the doctor gave me a leaflet as I was leaving and said: 'Read this when you get home. It will help.' It didn't help my *SP*, but at least it did make me realise I now had some strange type pf Phobia.

I still have that leaflet, now going yellow with age, and I have to say the description it gives for the condition is as true today as it was back then. The pity is that no way does it get across the full horror and misery of *SP*.

I reproduce it here for your interest.

Social Phobia

Social Phobia starts in childhood or, at the latest, the teenage years, but may not become severe until later in life. The phobia strikes both men and women equally. Three per cent of the population of Great Britain are affected so badly that they cannot lead a normal life. Victims have an extreme fear of all social situations, no matter how small or unimportant those occasions may be. They fear embarrassing themselves or being shown up in public. They constantly feel needless anxiety when they have to attend a social function, and will do anything to avoid meeting people, going to a party or for an interview, or eating in public places such as restaurants, cafés and bars. They feel the need to escape to the safety of their home, and to be alone or with someone they love who understands their overwhelming fear. In its most severe form, social phobia will result in a person living in complete social isolation for the rest of his or her life.

ECT (Electro-Convulsive Therapy)

We all recall the Jack Nicholson movie, *One Flew Over the Cuckoo's Nest.* From where I was sitting in the cinema, it was a very accurate and true-to-life portrait of how it is – or let's be charitable and say, how it was – when *SP* first hit me.

Don't get the idea that ECT is hardly used today; it is, and often.

One great improvement is that these days they use very advanced muscle relaxants that prevent the patient breaking his or her arms, legs or spine as a result of being put into an electrically induced seizure.

Not now maybe, but some years ago – back in the 1960s and '70s – I knew of cases where ECT was used as a means of controlling patients who had an illness (not *SP*) that made them prone to violent rages.

One condition that it's used for today is severe depression, when they suspect you may commit suicide, and several other severe and debilitating mental disorders.

There are different methods or ways of doing it, but – very briefly – you go into hospital for a couple of days. You have nothing to eat for 24 hours beforehand. Present will be a doctor, anaesthetist and nurse, and maybe also your psychiatrist. They put you to sleep, then give you an injection that paralyses your muscles. Electrodes are fixed to each temple and an electric current is passed through the brain, causing a seizure that lasts approximately a minute.

One doctor who wanted me to have ECT described it as having a 'mild fit in the brain'. This results in a change in the way the brain functions.

The experts are not sure how it works, but the claim is that you're not depressed anymore and feel much better. It has to be said that many patients say they suffer short-term memory loss and confusion after ECT (as, indeed, you will recall my friend Jack did), and many claim to feel as though they have changed as people, that they are just not the same person that they were. This is not surprising, as the seizure affects the entire brain, including the parts that control your thoughts and moods. Jack was to have the treatment twice a week for eleven weeks. According to medical experts, of all the treatments given under general anaesthetic, it's one of the safest; risk of death or injury is very low.

Tourette's Syndrome

This was the illness that Lisa suffered from and, as a direct result, she also had a form of *SP*.

The strange name comes from the French neuropsychiatrist who discovered it around 1890.

They say it's an inherited illness, but many sufferers, such as Lisa, can find no trace of it in their families.

The obvious symptoms are what they call "tics", where the person blinks constantly or jerks his or her head, or continually clears the throat or sniffs. In more severe forms, the person will shout out in public a long rambling dialogue of meaningless rubbish or abusive remarks, using swearwords. This can, of course, get the person into all sorts of embarrassing, and sometimes dangerous, situations. This in turn, understandably, can lead to someone avoiding any social occasion.

It is now thought that an abnormal metabolism of the neurotransmitters dopamine and serotonin is in some way connected with this condition.

The main form of treatment is medication. Research continues, but at present there is no cure.

It's very hard to live with, but sufferers do – with help

and support – win through. A person's intelligence or mental ability is not affected in any way.

Lobotomy

A lobotomy is a type of brain surgery in which the nerves in the front section – that's the frontal lobe of the brain – are cut. This, in theory, should reduce the intense anxiety a patient feels.

There is the risk of very severe far-reaching and unpredictable after-effects to this operation, including being unable to control bladder and bowel functions, and also very marked changes in behaviour and personality.

The operation became very popular in the medical world – but not with the patients – during the 1940s in America, when more than 50,000 patients, including some of the rich and powerful in society, were lobotomised.

Rosemary, sister of President Kennedy, had a frontal lobotomy to help with her depression. It was a complete failure. After the lobotomy she was totally unable to care for herself and needed 24-hour nursing, so she was put by her father, who had been the American Ambassador to Britain, into a convent where she spent the rest of her life.

In 1943, Rose, sister of playwright Tennessee Williams, had a lobotomy after suffering a nervous breakdown. As a result, she was disabled for life. Tennessee Williams was so saddened at having suggested the operation on the advice of a psychiatrist that he turned to drink and became an alcoholic, ever after advising people to 'stay away from psychiatry because it was a government-backed social belief system, not a medical science'.

The procedure was known then as the "ice pick lobotomy" because it involved literally pushing an ice pick type instrument into the brain via the eye socket. The practice spread worldwide, and in some countries was even used to control difficult children and was used routinely on troublesome convicts.

Dr. Egaz Moniz was one of the leading advocates of this operation and in 1949 was awarded the Nobel prize for his lobotomy techniques. One of his ex-patients was not so pleased with the after-effects that he'd suffered, stating that Moniz had condemned him to a living death, and when Moniz left the hospital late one night he shot him. The bullet lodged in his spine, and Moniz was confined to a wheelchair and unable to work for the rest of his life.

The lobotomies of the 1940s, '50s and '60s are now regarded as a shameful time in medical history; the procedure became less common with the advent of tranquilisers.

Lobotomy in itself is not a thing of the past and is still carried out today, but only as a last resort in chronic mental conditions that have been present for many years and have not responded to any other treatment.

In today's psychosurgical operations, laser or radiation is used to make tiny lesions in the brain; other treatments are radioactive implants, proton beams and ultrasonic waves.

Surveys suggest that, when patients are very carefully selected, the therapeutic success rate after psychosurgery is between 50 and 60 per cent.

Lightning Source UK Ltd.
Milton Keynes UK
UKHW040739090519
342383UK00001B/439/P